PARENTAL INVOLVEMENT

ABOUT THE AUTHOR

George R. Taylor, Ph.D., is Professor of Special Education and Chairperson of the Department of Special Education at Coppin State College, Baltimore, Maryland and CORE faculty, The Union Institute. Dr. Taylor has made significant contributions to the professional literature in the area of special education through research and publication. Additionally, he has served as a consultant on the local level to parental groups involved with disabled individuals.

PARENTAL INVOLVEMENT

A Practical Guide for Collaboration and Teamwork for Students with Disabilities

By

GEORGE TAYLOR

Coppin State College
Core Faculty
Union Institute

Charles C Thomas
PUBLISHER • LTD.
SPRINGFIELD • ILLINOIS • U.S.A.

Published and Distributed Throughout the World by

CHARLES C THOMAS • PUBLISHER, LTD.
2600 South First Street
Springfield, Illinois 62794-9265

©*2000 by* CHARLES C THOMAS • PUBLISHER, LTD.

ISBN 0-398-07071-7 (cloth)
ISBN 0-398-07072-5 (paper)

Library of Congress Catalog Card Number: 00-023451

With THOMAS BOOKS *careful attention is given to all details of man-*
ufacturing and design. It is the Publisher's desire to present books that are sat-
isfactory as to their physical qualities and artistic possibilities and appropri-
ate for their particular use. THOMAS BOOKS *will be true to those laws*
of quality that assure a good name and good will.

Printed in the United States of America
CR-R-3

Library of Congress Cataloging-in-Publication Data

Taylor, George R.
    Parental involvement : a practical guide for collaboration and
teamwork for students with disabilities / by George Taylor.
        p.cm
    Includes bibliographical references and index.
    ISBN 0-398-07071-7 (cloth) -- ISBN 0-398-07072-5 (paper)
    1. Special education--Parent participation--United States. 2.
Handicapped children--Education--United States. I. Title.

LC3981 .T384 2000
371.9--dc21   00-023451

PREFACE

Considerable attention has been given to parental involvement in education during the last decade. Factors responsible for the increase include federal and state legislation, and national parental groups and organizations. The movement has empowered parents and has given them a legal and moral right to be involved as partners in collaboration with the schools and community agencies in the education of their children.

It is generally recognized how parental reactions to their children with disabilities may be crucial to their adjustment as well as to the nature and type of interventions and adjustments needed by their children to successfully adjust in school and cope in adult life. In many instances, both parents and children may need psychological intervention. Some suggested strategies have been outlined in the text.

The text provides a collaborative model which parents, teachers, and community agencies may employ to meet the needs of children with disabilities. Specific activities and intervention strategies provide an approach for parents and teachers to jointly develop programs. Each will have equal responsibilities and rights in the process.

The first chapter discusses the impact of children with disabilities on parenting, and an overview of parental involvement in the schools. The impact of societal conditions and federal state legislation upon parental involvement is fully explored. Chapter 2 discusses the need for parenting skills and some recommended strategies to employ to aid in the adjustment of children with disabilities. The importance of parental reactions to their children with disabilities and their perceptions toward the disability are explored in Chapter 3. Chapter 4 discusses the need for counseling parents of children with disabilities. Specific strategies and techniques are summarized. The importance of federal legislation on parental involvement is stressed in chapter 5. Major aspects of the law mandating parental involvement are highlighted. Chapter 6 is devoted to techniques for improving parental involvement in the total school program. Working with families from diverse cultures and strategies for promoting diversity are summarized in chapter 7. Innovative ways of jointly sharing information and ensuring confidentiality of information are pinpointed in Chapter 8. Ways of reporting information to parents are discussed in Chapter 9. Chapter 10 is devoted to discussing parents as resources in the school. Strategies are discussed for promoting parental involvement. Parental perceptions on inclusion are reported in Chapter 11. Recent research findings are summarized to reflect parental perceptions. Chapter 12 outlines some projections in parental involvement during the next two decades.

This text was written to provide information to parents and educators that may be applied to minimize the effects of parents having children with disabilities in their families, as well as providing strategies for educators to employ in educating children with disabilities. The major thrust was to indicate how parents, teachers, and community agencies could collaborate in providing appropriate services and strategies to children with disabilities.

Many of the materials obtained in this text are a direct result of in-service presentations, consultancies with public schools and private agencies, teaching in-service teachers, and research projects dealing with collaborative projects involving parents of children with disabilities.

G.T.

ACKNOWLEDGMENTS

Compiling this text was not an individual effort. It would have been impossible to complete this awesome task without the assistance of others.

A special thanks is given to the graduate students I have taught at Coppin State College for their suggestions and feedback for encouragement during compiling the information needed for developing this text and to Mrs. Emma Crosby for her sincere commitment and dedication in typing the final manuscript.

I also wish to acknowledge the assistance provided by the staff of Charles C Thomas. Their assistance was instrumental in producing the final copy of the text.

CONTENTS

PARENTAL INVOLVEMENT

Chapter 1

A SYSTEMS PERSPECTIVE OF HUMAN DEVELOPMENT

INTRODUCTION

From a systems perspective of human development, the way an individual acts is a product of the interactions that occur between a person and his or her environment. This section will examine recent developments in family system theory related to the interactions within families and the interactions between families and professionals.

Family systems theory provides a framework for understanding what a family is and how it functions. It also provides professionals with a model of how to collaborate with families. Turnbull and Turnbull (1996) described three assumptions that are central to family systems theory. They are: (1) the input/output configuration of the system, (2) the concept of wholeness and subsystems, and (3) the role of boundaries in defining systems (Whitechurch & Constantine as cited in Turnbull & Turnbull, 1996). The first assumption explains how the inputs (family characteristics) interact with the system to produce outputs (family function). For example, when a child with disabilities is born (family characteristics), this places a new set of stresses on the family and may change how family members interact with each other and with individuals outside of the family (family function). The second assumption is that the system must be understood as a whole and cannot be understood by examining only its component parts (Whitechurch & Constantine as cited in Turnbull & Turnbull, 1996). For example, it follows from this assumption that it is necessary to understand the family and understand the child. Finally, the third assumption is that family subsystems are separated by boundaries that are created by the interaction of family members within the family unit and with outside influences. For example, the boundaries set with professionals are likely to be different from the ones set with family members.

Much of the knowledge about the changes in the relationships between parents and professionals that have occurred during the past 25 years can be attributed to the work done by Bronfenbrenner. He stressed that parenting behavior is influenced by environmental factors that are both internal to and external to the family. These parenting behaviors then influence the child's behavior. For example, Bronfenbrenner (1979, as cited in Dunst, Trivette, Hamby, & Pollock, 1990) stated that

> whether parents can perform effectively in their child-rearing roles within the family depends on role demands, stresses, and supports emanating from other settings. Parents' evaluations of their own capacity to function, as well as their view of their child, are related to such external factors as flexibility of job schedules, adequacy of child care arrangements, the presence of friends and neighbors who can help out in large and small emergencies, the quality of health and social services, and neighborhood safety.

This quotation emphasizes the role that outside influences can have on families. Recognizing that role has been a critical factor affecting many of the changes that have occurred in the parent-professional relationship. It is important for anyone working with families to have an understanding of family systems theory because it provides a framework for understanding families in an individualized and personalized way. Professionals who possess such an understanding are more likely to be attuned to the families and their strengths, expectations, priorities, and needs. Such an understanding in turn leads to a more effective and collaborative relationship with families—and families are most able to promote students' positive educational results (Turnbull & Turnbull, 1996).

It is evident from the above analysis that significant social changes have occurred between families and the professionals (see Table 1).

Table 1
SOCIAL CHANGES: A MODEL FOR PARENT-TEACHER COLLABORATION

Factors	1950s	1990s
Family	Extended, traditional nuclear	Neolocal nuclear
Neighborhood	Personal, cohesive	Impersonal, multicultural
Neighbors	Concerned, responsible, active	Concerned, defensive, passive, or indirectly active
Companions/friends	Close, cohesive, socially and emotionally supportive	Often distant or unavailable, nonexistent for many needing social and emotional support
School	Small, in the neighborhood, personal	Large, outside the neighborhood, impersonal
Teachers	Accepted as friends, neighbors, community leaders	Perceived as strangers, professional, specialists
Knowledge	Limited, manageable within existing standards of behavior and application	Exploding, unmanageable within existing standards of behavior and application
Church Standards/values	Influential	Relatively less influential Relative, fragmented, emphasizing the bizarre and unacceptable.
Work	Simple, personal, available, sufficient to produce needed goods, supportive of artisans	Mechanized, impersonal, automated, specialized, unavailable to many, less supportive of artisans
Material goods	Limited, emphasizing necessities for living	Available to majority, emphasizing luxuries

Mobility	Limited for most people	Nearly unlimited
Communication/ transportation	Limited, slow, inefficient	Nearly limited, rapid, more efficient
National and world	Not widely followed or understood events	Extensively followed and understood

The challenges appear to be very positive in that they have promoted improved collaboration between the families and the professionals. Chapters 9 and 11 provide additional insight into collaborations.

IMPACT OF THE DISABILITY ON PARENTING

There is a preponderance of research on the impact of a child with a disability on parenting (see Chapter 2). Studies have covered the gamut of disabilities and have indicated what adaptations and modifications parents should make to meet the needs of various types of disabilities (Alpher & Schloss, 1994; Bradley, Knoll, & Agosta, 1992; Lian & Aloia, 1994; Stoneman & Berman, 1993; Turnbull & Turnbull, 1990; Green & Shinn, 1995; Shea & Bauer, 1991; Westling, 1996).

Data in Table 1 reflect the many collaborative social changes between parents and professionals over the last four decades. Social changes have significantly changed to aid parents of children with disabilities.

The majority of research in this area indicated that parenting involves many complex processes from the birth of a child through adulthood. For parents of children with disabilities, the process is more pronounced and prolonged. The impact of children with disabilities on the family structure is dynamic. Interactions and collaborations between the various family members can be adversely affected by the present of a disabled child in the family. In many cases, the family structure will need to be adapted and modified. In the process of change, many parents will need professional advice, services, and information. (Refer to Chapters 3 and 4 for additional information on the impact of a child with disability on the family.)

Individuals with disabilities, as well as all children, follow developmental milestones in all areas of growth. Parents will need professional information in these areas. Professional information will assist parents in working with their children where there are developmental problems and to pattern the learning of skills in a more predictable manner. It is commonly agreed that parents should be provided with as much information as possible concerning their disabled children. Heddel (1988) recommended the following guidelines relevant to communicating diagnostic information to parents:

- Parents should be told as soon as possible, preferably by a doctor. This information should be communicated in an appropriate place, such as an interview room or office.
- There should be no casual observers–this is a private matter.
- Both parents should be told at the same time. It should not be left to one parent to inform the other.
- The newborn should also be in the room, if possible.
- Parents should be given time and opportunity to ask questions, even though they may be confused and at a loss for words.
- Another interview should be scheduled, not more than a day or two later. Parents should be encouraged to bring questions that will inevitably come up in the interim and should be told that other persons having experience in the specific type of disability will be at the next meeting to help answer questions and suggest sources of help. Information is also needed on strategies that parents can employ in working with their disabled children at home.

OVERVIEW OF PARENTAL INVOLVEMENT IN THE SCHOOLS

Parents were instrumental in developing schools in the early centuries of the country. They provided the climate for the creation of public schools. They formed organizations to raise laws to build schools, and petitioned legislators to pass laws to build, construct, and support public schools. Historical, parental input was sought and encouraged in the early formation of public schools. Unfortunately, the movement to create public schools did not include disabled children. Formulation of public schools was premised on the concept that they were developed for "normal children." This concept prevailed well into the 20th century.

During the early part of the 20th century, society's understanding of disability increased due chiefly to advances and research in all areas of human functioning. Specialized provisions were made for educating children with disabilities. Attitudes and concepts concerning disability began to change due to increased research in all aspects or disabilities, the affects of World Wars I and II, federal and state legislation, and the rise of national parental groups (Mallory, 1996).

Impact of Research

Research in the fields of biochemistry, medicine, psychology, sociology, education, and other allied disciplines has added immeasurably to our understanding, treatment, and the reduction of many types of disabilities. Many disabled children who once died at birth or at an early age are now living due to medical breakthroughs. All types of medical interventions are being conducted. These efforts have resulted in many children with disabilities being saved.

Influences of World Wars I and II

The impact of World Wars I and II significantly changed the public's reactions toward disability. Many recruits who went into the service were normal in all aspects. They returned with all types of disabilities due to the trauma of war. Society readily began to realize that something had to be done for these recruits, since they were not responsible for their disabilities. This positive attitude toward treatment for these disabled recruits was captured by parents of children with disabilities and they began to demand treatment for their disabled children.

Formation of National Parental Groups

Parents formed national advocacy groups such as the Association for Retarded Citizens and the Association for Children and Adults with Learning Disabilities. These are a few examples (see Appendix A for additional associations). These groups have asserted the rights of disabled individuals in the courts and at state and congressional hearings. They have been instrumental in lobbying for the rights of disabled individuals. Due to their efforts, much federal and state legislation passed may be attributed to them.

Role of Federal Legislation

Federal legislation has significantly improved the educational opportunities for children with disabilities. As indicated, parents were instrumental in having these federal mandates passed. Section 504 of the Vocational Act of 1973, prohibited the discrimination of children with disabilities. The Congress of the United States aided school districts to comply with Section 504 by passing the Education for All Handicapped Children Act, Public Law 94-142. PL 94-142 specifies how Section 504 guidelines should be implemented. Parental involvement in the referral, identification, placement, programming, and evaluation phases of each child's individual education is a major thrust of that law (National Council on Disability, 1995; U.S. Department of Education, 1995).

TRENDS IN PARENTAL PARTICIPATION

Today, parents of children with disabilities are not as actively involved as they were historically. Several reasons may attribute to the decline of parental involvement in the schools. The basic family structure has changed, which was so prevalent in the early years the structure is not present today. Some parents do not feel welcome in the schools; a significant number of minority parents who do not speak fluent English are present in our society (this issue is addressed in Chapter 7). The economic conditions have forced both parents to work or, in the case of a one-parent family, the parent must work two jobs to support the family. Some parents are critical of the performance of their children in public schools as measured by standardized tests and have called for reforms in education (Finders & Lewis, 1994; Harry & McLaughlin, 1995).

These factors have also had an impact on parents of disabled children as well. However, due to federal legislation, parental involvement in the public schools has escalated due chiefly to The Family Education Rights and Privacy Act which was passed in 1974. Chapter 5 has been devoted to a discussion of the impact of federal legislation on parental involvement.

PARENTAL CONCERNS

Concerns of parents relevant to their children with disabilities cover a variety of issues. Generally, parents are concerned with the following:

1. Cause of the disability. What factors are responsible for the disability? Is it hereditary? What did we do to contribute to the condition? Why us? Why did that happen to us? Is it safe to have another child? Parents generally feel that they are responsible for the disability. They constantly seek reasons for the disability by visiting different professionals to establish the cause and a cure.

2. Impact on the family structure. Parents are concerned with how their child with a disability will impact upon the family. Will his/her presence affect their normal children? How will the disability be explained to the children, relatives, and neighbors? Are there educational and community resources available to serve my child?

3. Treatment and intervention. Many parents spend countless hours seeking treatment or a cure for the disability. Questions posed by parents may include the following: Is there some type of surgery which may assist my child? What type of treatments or interventions are recommended? Where may the needed services be located? Is drug therapy recommended? What type of community services are available? How will his/her school placement be determined?

4. Prognostic outlook. Parents are deeply concerned with the future for their children. Questions and concerns frequently voiced are: Will a cure be found for our children? Will our children outgrow the disability? What will our children be like when they are adults? What are the chances if we have other children that they will not be disabled?

The four broad areas outlined are by no way a comprehensive review of all parental concerns. These broad areas only reflect basic concerns of parents. (Chapter 3 comprehensively address parental reactions and concerns.) Additionally, these categories can be subdivided into additional areas. One of the major purposes of this text is to fully investigate the aforementioned areas and to present research to answer the many questions posed by parents of children with disabilities (Green & Shinn, 1995; Bailey, Star, Turnbull, & Turnbull, 1995).

SUMMARY

Family systems theory provides a framework for understanding the dynamics that are present within families. Children with disabilities and their families face a unique set of issues, as well as the usual challenges of childhood. Understanding the issues that are important to families is particularly critical when trying to develop a positive relationship between professionals and families. Both formal and informal avenues for collaboration exist. However, open communication is the integral component of developing this important collaborative relationship. In order to improve a collaborative relationship, parents must avail themselves of the training offered at family service centers. Some of the recommended training would include:

1. Parenting skills
2. Counseling skills
3. Strategies for coping with their disabled children
4. Legal rights and due process procedures
5. Sharing information
6. Collaborative strategies
7. Sharing information
8. Strategies for involvement in the school
9. Promoting cultural awareness
10. Reporting strategies

The organization of the text is premised upon the listed areas. These areas will be fully developed and specifically outlined to assist parents and educators to effective collaborative activities to promote their children's education, as well as deal effectively with problems which they may encounter in society. Additionally, the text is designed to: (1) assist parents to recognize and accept their children's disabilities, (2) develop positive attitudes toward their disabled children, (3) identify and recognize resources and treatment facilities in the community, (4) recognize the importance of counseling, (5) work in collaboration with the school and community agencies, and (6) deal effectively with their own frustration and self-esteem.

REFERENCES

Affleck, G., & Tennen, M. (1993). Cognitive adaptation to adversity: Insights from parents of medically fragile infants. In A.P. Turnbull, J. M. Patterson, S. K. Behr, D. L. Murphy, D. L. Marguis, & M. J. Blue-Banning (Eds.) *Cognitive coping, families and disability*. Baltimore: Paul H. Brooks.

Alper, S., & Schloss, K. (Eds.) (1994). *Families of students with disabilities*. Boston: Allyn and Bacon.

Bailey, D. B., Palsha, S. A., & Simeonsson, R. J. (1991). Professional skills, concerns, and perceived importance of work with families in early intervention. *Exceptional Children, 58*(2), 156-165.

Bradley, V. J., Knoll, J., & Agosta, J. M. (1992). *Emerging issues in family support*. Washington, DC: The American Association on Mental Retardation.

Dunst, C. J., Trivette, C. M., Hamby, D., & Pollock, B. (1990). Family systems correlates the behavior of young children with handicaps. *Journal of Early Intervention, 14*(3), 204-218.

Findes, M., & Lewis, C. (1994). Why some parents don't come to school. *Educational Leadership, 51*(8), 50-54.

Green, S. K., & Shinn, M. R. (1995). Parent attitudes about special education and reintegration: What is the role of student results. *Exceptional Children, 6*(3), 269-281.

Harry, B., Allen, N., & McLaughlin, M. (1995). Communication versus compliance: African American parents involvement in special education. *Exceptional Children, 61*(4), 364-377.

Heddel, F. (1988). *Children with mental handicaps*. Ramsbury, Marlborough, England: Crewood Press.

Lian, M. J., & Aolia, G. (1994). Parental responses, roles, and responsibilities. In S. K. Alper, P. J. Schlass, & C. N. Schloss (Eds.), *Families of students with disabilities*. Boston: Allyn and Bacon.

Mallory, B. L. (1996). The role of social policy in the life cycle transitions. *Exceptional Children, 62*(3), 213-223.

Morningstaf, M. E., Turnbull, A. P., & Turnbull, H. R. (1995). What do students with disabiliites tell us about the importance of involvement in the transition from school to adult life. *Exceptional Children, 62*(3), 249-260.

National Council on Disabiliity. (1995). Improving the implementation of the individuals with Disabilites Education Act: Making schools work for all America's children. Washington, DC: Author.

Shea, T., & Bauer, A. M. (1991). *Parents and teachers of children with exceptionalities: A handbook for collaboration*. Boston: Allyn and Bacon.

Stoneman, Z., & Berman, P. W. (1993). *The effects of mental retardation, disability, and illness on sibling relationships*. Baltimore: Paul H. Brooks.

Turnbull, A. P., & Turnbull, H. R. (1990). *Families, professionals, and exceptinality: A special partership* (2nd ed.). Columbus, OH: Merrill.

Turnbull, A. P., Turnbull, H. R., & Shankon, L. D. (1995). *Exceptional lives: Special education in today's schools*. Englewood Cliffs, NJ: Merrill.

Turnbull, A. P., & Turnbull, H. R. (1996). *Families, professionals, and exceptionality.* Upper Saddle River, NJ: Merrill.

U. S. Department of Education. (1995). *Individuals with Disabilities Education Act Amendments of 1995.* Washington, DC: Author.

Westling, D. C. (1996). What do parents with moderate and severe mental disabilities want? *Education and Training in Mental Retardation and Development Disabilites, 21,* 86-114.

Whitechurch, G. G., & Constantine, L. L. (1993). Systems theory. In P. G. Boss, W. J. Doherty, R. LaRossa, W. R. Schumm, & S. K. Steinmetz (Eds.), *Sourcebook of family theory and methods: A contextual approach* (pp. 325-352). New York: Plenum.

Winston, P. J. (1994). Families of children with disabilities. In H. G. Haring, L. McCormick, & T. G. Haring (Eds.), *Exceptional children and youth* (6th ed.). New York: Merrill.

Chapter 2

PARENTING SKILLS

INTRODUCTION

The importance of parenting cannot be overlooked by the schools. Parents are the child's first teachers. The parental role in the family therefore focuses on being a role model for the child. In the early formative stage of a child, the actions of parents or adults are modeled by children. It is at this point in a child's life that the quality of parental behavior is critical. Parents, who express warmth, happiness, consideration, and respect in their daily handling of the child are acknowledged to be assisting the child in developing a positive approach to life. Parents should provide model behaviors that they wish their children to demonstrate (Dunst, Trivette, Hamby, & Pollock, 1990). If parents do not provide guidance by personal example of their major values, it is difficult to help a child emulate desired behaviors (Cullingford, 1996).

In essence, behaviors parents wish their children to exhibit in their adult lives should be a reflection of their own behaviors. The primary parental role in the family is that of being a teacher of trust. Quite often, society has witnessed many children who have no confidence in their families or themselves; hence they choose alternate support groups as a family. Parents need to have confidence that giving emotional support to their children will enable them to cope with the demands of family, friends, school, and society.

Dealing with the confidential aspect of the child's life is one of the most essential arts of parenting. At this time, children are taught to have confidence and reliance on themselves. Parents are advised to intervene in whatever practicable way to influence their children's behavior; to set limits, shape behaviors, and engage in mental problem solving discussions (White, Church, & Constantine, 1993).

14

Parenting, therefore, requires parents to provide skills which will equip their children to function appropriately in society.

Parenting is not about beautiful things all the time. It is about good and bad, the fulfilling and draining, the rewarding and the punishing. With respect to this, parenting practically depends on how well parents grow with their children and help their children to become positive individuals. To build this confidence, parents need to exhibit self-confidence in the presence of their children.

Respect is a major art of parenting. Parenting is a most stimulating job that requires wisdom, sensitivity, strength, and endurance. To be effective, parents must respect their children as human beings. In some cases, children turn to undesirable elements because their parents do not set appropriate models for them to emulate. The mind-set of children is conditioned primarily by how their parents respect or regard them (Caldwell, 1997).

Children need to be interacted with and talked to with as much respect, courtesy, and consideration as you would expect for oneself. Yelling at children has a deteriorating effect on them. To receive respect and cooperation from children, parents should respect their individual rights.

Love and discipline are among other arts of parenting. Although, it is advisable for parents to love their children, it must be expressed in ways that are beneficial for their children and comfortable for the parents. Discipline is a form of love, and parents should learn how to use it to avoid letting love for the child cloud the responsibility of parenting.

Communication is a form of parenting. Parents who communicate well with their children create, in a practical form, a direct channel for closeness and development of a positive self-concept which will be needed for later school success (Solo, 1997). Children who experience all or part of the aforementioned develop confidence about themselves that carries over to many other situations or difficulties that they may face. A woman who experienced good communication and a warm relationship with her own parents always looks forward with confidence to her own mothering, and there is every likelihood that she will pass her good experience on to her children.

The importance of parenting in this family relies on commitments, providing warmth and nurturing for all members, and encouraging the development of difficulties. The challenge in parenting is to relate to children with disabilities, as well as to children without disabilities, in manners and ways that stimulate their potentialities for growth and provide appropriate opportunities for experiences that develop these potentialities. Parenting skills in various cultures differ. Educators and teachers should be aware of the various culture styles and adjust instructional programs and school activities to reflect diversity (Hindle, 1998; Okagaki & French, 1998; Taylor, 1997).

DEVELOPING PRO-SOCIAL SKILLS/BEHAVIORS

Research from social learning theory implies that pro-social learning theory implies that pro-social behaviors of children with disabilities are enhanced when behavioral expectations are clearly specified and reinforced with praise, encouragement, and other positive acts by parents and teachers. (Refer to Table 2 for specific examples.)

Table 2
NINETY-TWO (92) WAYS TO PROMOTE ACADEMIC AND SOCIAL GROWTH OF CHILDREN WITH DISABILITIES

1. You're doing a good job?
2. You did a lot of work today!
3. Now you've figure it out.
4. That's RIGHT!!!
5. Now you've got the hang of it!
6. That's the way!
7. You're doing fine!
8. Now you have it!
9. Nice going.
10. You're really going to town.
11. That's great
12. You did it that time.
13. GREAT!
14. FANTASTIC!
15. TERRIFIC!
16. Good for you.
17. GOOD WORK!
18. That's better.
19. EXCELLENT!
20. Good job, (name of student)
21. You outdid yourself today.
22. That's the best you've done ever.
23. Good going.
24. That's really nice.
25. Keep it up!
26. WOW!!
27. Keep up the good work.
28. Much better.
29. Good for you.
30. That's much better.
31. Good thinking.
32. Marvelous
33. Exactly right!
34. SUPER!
35. Nice going!
36. You make it look easy.
37. Way to go.
38. Superb!!
39. You're getting better every day.
40. WONDERFUL!
41. I knew you could do it.
42. Keep working on it, your getting better!
43. You're doing beautifully.
44. You're really working hard today.
45. That's the way to do it.

46. Keep on trying.
47. That's it.
48. You've got it made.
49. You're very good at that.
50. You're learning fast.
51. I'm very proud of you.
52. You certainly did well today.
53. That's good.
54. I'm happy to see you working like that.
55. I'm proud of the way you worked today.
56. That's the right way to do it.
57. You're really learning a lot.
58. That's better than ever.
59. That's quite an improvement.
60. That kind of work makes me very happy.
61. Now you've figured it out.
62. PERFECT!
63. FINE!!!
64. That's IT!
65. You figured that out fast.
66. You remembered.
67. You're really improving.
68. I think you've got it now.
69. Well look at you go.
70. TREMENDOUS!
71. OUTSTANDING!
72. No that's what I call a fine job.
73. You did that very well.
74. That was first-class work.
75. Right on.
76. SENSATIONAL!!
77. That's the best ever.
78. Good remembering.
79. You haven't missed a thing.
80. You really make my job fun.
81. You must have been practicing.
82. You got it made.
83. Good show.
84. CONGRATULATIONS!
85. Not bad.
86. Nice going (name of student)
87. OUTSTANDING!
88. SUPERIOR!
89. Good thinking.
90. Clever.
91. Perfect.
92. Keep up the good work.

Table 2 provides some ways in which parents and teachers may promote academic and social growth, as well as raising the self-esteem of all children, including children with disabilities. Table 2 shows 92 ways for saying to children with disabilities that they have done a good job. These words and phrases are designed to reinforce good work habits and develop skills needed for academic and social success. Data in Table 2 is in concert with principles advocated by Bandura (1997). Bandura's social learning theory advocates how social learning may aid parents in using parental skills.

Bandura proposed a very comprehensive and powerful social learning theory of modeling. Bandura's theory stands as the most popular theory of modeling today. One reason his theory is so popular is that it explicitly recognized that children imitate only a small fraction of all the responses they learn through observation. According to Bandura, children learn a multitude of brand new social responses simply by observing the actions of significant and salient models around them, including their parents, siblings, teachers, and playmates. Bandura calls this process observational learning and believes that this is a major way children acquire new patterns of social behavior. This theory fits into what most developmental psychologist say: that from 0-7 children are learning from significant others, and from seven to early teenage years they are modeling and demonstrating whey they have learned from others. During the teenage years, when children are looking for their own identity, they are looking to their friends and others in the same developmental stage for learning. If parents use their skills surrounding discipline and rewards during formative years, they still will be able to lovingly guide their children to adulthood without serious irreversible traumatic experiences. On the other hand, without parents employing good parenting skills, children may develop unacceptable social skills (Taylor, 1998).

Social learning theory implies that children learn from instruction and discipline they directly experience at the hands of their parents, teachers, and other socializing agents. Parents must give instruction to their children, establish routines, and serve as role models until their children have developed acceptable behaviors. Parents must decide when it is appropriate to transfer the locus of control from themselves to their children. Before transfer occurs, parents should be sure that their children have shown appropriate self-directed strategies to make independent decisions and to act appropriately on their own (Coleman, 1986).

EFFECTIVE PARENTING SKILLS STRATEGIES

Parenting is the process that develops skills needed for children to be successful in their environments. In order for parenting skills to be successful, parents need to be cognizant of techniques to employ, involving trust, respect, love, discipline, and communication. The recommended parenting skills for parents to use in directing and guiding their children with disabilities have been developed premised upon the aforementioned techniques (Naeef, 1997; Dunst, Trivette, & Hamby, 1990; Winton, 1994; Powell, 1998; Leung, 1998).

Parents believe that they naturally know how to raise their children but, unfortunately, humans are not born preprogrammed with those child-rearing skills that will naturally help them to accurately discriminate and discern what to do when they confront a two-year-old's no's, or a seven-year-old's defiance about doing his or her homework, or a teenager's rebelliousness about obeying curfew set by the city to protect him or her from physical harm.

Parenting skills are not taught. Parents learn these skills through trial and error, strategies from their parents, information from published sources, and from specialists in the field. Parents generally use information from these sources to guide and direct the activities of their children. This is equally true for parents of children with disabilities. Most social sciences agree that parenting is a complex and dynamic process (Giannetti & Sagarese, 1997).

Whereas there is no universal set of principles for teaching parents parenting skills, parents must respond to the physical, psychological, and social/emotional needs of their children if they are to be successful in school and society. According to Taylor (1998), during the formative years, parents can promote positive and effective parenting skills of their children with disabilities through implementing the following strategies.

Recommended Strategies

1. Related Tasks to the Developmental Level of the Child. Some children are eager for new tasks and experiences. Others need to be coaxed and encouraged. Regardless of how your child approaches challenges, success will be important for the development of self-concept. Direct your child toward challenges that he or she is developmentally ready for. Break down big tasks into smaller parts (e.g., if your child wants to make a garden, break down the project into easy steps—digging, making holes, dropping seeds, covering them, watering). Show the child each step, but let your child do it for himself/herself.

2. Build a Sense of Security and Trust. Given a loving and responsive home environment, your child will be able to establish a sense of self apart from the people and things about him/her. Patience, consistency, and loving discipline are acts of caring which support your child as he/she strives toward independence.

3. Be Sensitive to Your Child's Signals. As an individual, your child shows unique ways of responding to new people and new experiences. Although he/she may not be able to put his/her feelings into words, he/she may need your reassurance when entering into unknown territory. Sometimes fearfulness and negative behaviors are signs that your child is not quite ready for the challenge at hand.

4. Make Your Child an Equal in the Family. Membership in a family involves learning to share: 1sharing time, sharing material resources, and sharing one another's life. As your child grows more capable, he/she should be given the opportunity to perform tasks which contribute to the functioning of the family. Your child also needs to be shown ways to express how much he/she cares about the people that he/she loves.

5. Be Aware of Your Child's Limitations. Realize that your child's present capabilities are largely determined by his/her overall developmental level. Your expectations of his/her behaviors should be based on his/her developmental age, not chronological age.

6. Go from the Known to the Unknown. Prepare your child for new experiences by linking the familiar to the unknown. If your child has met the librarian and visited the children's room in the neighborhood library many times, then participation in preschool story hour is not so scary a prospect.

SUMMARY

From the very beginning, children with disabilities should have an important place within the family structure. By being responsive to children's needs, the foundation for interactive social relationships begins. The drive for independence emerges as developmental skills grow. As your child tries to do more and more for himself/herself, he/she continues to depend on you for guidance and support. Parents' delight in the small accomplishments of a child can set expectations for larger success.

Parents of individuals with disabilities, as well as all parents, have a tremendous influence and impact on setting appropriate models for developing SOCIAL AND ACADEMIC SKILLS. The developmental level of the child, as well as developmental sequence of tasks, must be considered in social and academic training. Parents can contribute significantly to their disabled children's self-concept and control through appropriate modeling strategies.

In order for parents of individuals with disabilities to be effective change agents in promoting appropriate social and academic skills development, early intervention in health care, counseling, housing, nutrition, education, and child reading practices, etc. must be improved. Early intervention and parental involvement are essential for preparing children to master skill and tasks successfully.

Parental involvement is a must in the lives of children. A thorough review of the relevant literature reveals that: (1) parenting is essential for the proper nurturing and caring of children and (2) that it is essential for nourishing, protecting, guiding, and social learning that must accompany a child throughout life, through the course of development.

REFERENCES

Bandura, A. (1997). Social learning: Child-rearing practices and their effect. In G. David, & R. Busey (Eds.), *Social development* (pp. 79-85). Englewood Cliffs, NJ: Prentice Hall.

Caldwell, L. (1997). Tips to parents from your pre-schooler. *Child Care Information Exchange, 113*, 89.

Coleman, M. C. (1986). *Behavior disorders: Theory and practice.* Englewood Cliffs, NJ: The Free Press.

Cullingford, C. (1996). The reality of childhood. *Time Educational Supplement, 4193*, 15.

Dunst, G. J., Trivette, C. M., Hamby, D., & Pollock, B. (1990). Family systems correlates the behavior of young children with handicaps. *Journal of Early Intervention, 14* (3), 204-218.

Giannetti, C., & Sagarese, M. (1992). *The roller-coaster years: Raising your child through the maddening yet magical middle school years.* New York: Broadway Books.

Hindle, J. S. (1998). Parenting in different cultures: Time to focus. *Developmental Psychology, 34* (4), 698-700.

Leung, K. (1998). Parenting styles and academic achievement: A cross-cultural study. *Merrill-Palmer Quaterly, 44* (2), 157-172.

Naeef, R. A. (1997). Special children challenged parents: The struggles and rewards of rasing a child with a disability. *Exceptional Parents, 27*, 21.

Okagaki, L., & French, P. A. (1998). Parenting and children's school achievement: A multiethnic perspective. *American Educational Research Journal, 25*, 123-144.

Powell, D. R. (1998). Re-weaving parents into early childhood education programs. *Education Digest, 64* (3), 22-25.

Solo, L. (1997). School success begins at home. *Principal, 77* (2), 29-30.

Taylor, G. R. (1997). *Curriculum strategies: Social skills intervention for young African American males.* Westport, Connecticut: Praeger.

Whitechurch, G. G., & Constantine, L. L. (1993). System theory. In P. G. Boss, W. J. Doherty, R. LaRossa, W. R. Schumm, S. K. Steinmitz (Eds.), *Sourcebook of family theory and methods: A contextual approach.* New York: Plenam.

Winton, P. D. (1994). Families of children with disabilities. In N. G. Haring, L. McCormick, & T. G. Haring (Eds.), *Exceptional children and youth* (6th ed.), (pp. 502-525). New York,: Merrill.

Chapter 3

PARENTAL REACTIONS

EMOTIONAL REACTIONS

Parents show and display a variety of reactions to their children with disabilities (Seligman, 1991a). Some reactions are so severe until some parents need psychological intervention to cope with the situations. Some parents gradually accept the idea; however, few parents totally initially accept a child with a disability without some counseling.

The age of onset of the disability is an important factor to consider. The reaction of a parent of a child with a disability diagnosed in the fifth grade is likely to be uniquely different from that of a parent who learned after three months that the child was disabled. The manner in which data are shared with a parent can sufficiently influence parental reactions toward their children with disabilities. Information relevant to a childís disability should be shared with the parents in a friendly, warm, and professional manner, and the presenter should be sensitive to the feelings of the parents. Parents are also greatly concerned about the financial support needed to provide the necessary services for their children.

Many negative emotions may be generated from the parents concerning this issue. Parents not only react emotionally to their children with disabilities but also from pressures applied from the communityís perception of the disability. Frequently, the communityís perceptions of children with disabilities may cause parents to be rejected from or not feeling welcome to participate in many of the social clubs and functions. The reactions may lead to parents being isolated from the community (Clemens-Brower, 1997).

Parental emotional reactions to their children with disabilities differ greatly. Emotional reactions may range from acceptance through complete rejection of the child with a disability (Hynan, 1996). Some parents are mature enough, with minimum intervention, to accept the disability of their children. These parents attempt to provide services to aid their children.

Other parents tend to attempt to deny that their children have disabilities: They are constantly trying to find causes for the disability. They mount a continuous search to find ways in which the child may be made normal by sending him/her to various specialists to treat the disability. This type of reaction significantly impedes realistic planning for the child with a disability, since parents and family may not perceive the child as disabled, but hostile, not cooperating with the family, or plain lazy (Lian & Aloia, 1994).

Some parents (mostly males) are unable to face the reality of their childrens disabilities. They constantly deny that a disability exists. Many are not informed about the cause of the disability. They make believe that the disability is attributed to some past act that they have committed, or that it is due to inheritance. Training, education, treatment, and family relationships concerning children with disabilities are significantly affected by these reactions.

As in the case of any human being, children with disabilities do not live in a vacuum. A child with a disability needs, as do all children, a close emotional relationship with others and these relationships must be satisfying and stress-reducing if he/she is to achieve his/her maximum potentialities. Further, as with all children, the relationship between the child with a disability and his/her parents and community is of great importance. If the parents manifest negative personality reactions to the childs deficient abilities, then it becomes more difficult for wholesome relationships to be established. The greater the negative reactions of the parents, the less likely it is that the child will achieve the level of emotional maturity he/she is capable of attaining. Negative reactions of the parents, thus, can adversely affect the full maturational process of the child with a disability. It is of prime importance that any emotional problems which surface as a result of the child's disability be professionally treated on a continuous basis. Systematic treatment is highly recommended since the emotional development of the child is directly related to the positive reactions of the parents toward him/her (Harshman, 1996). It is commonly known that the future psychological adjustment of disabled children greatly depends upon the emotional climate projected by the parents within the home.

IMPACT OF REACTIONS ON THE FAMILY

When a child with a disability is born or when a non-disabled child becomes disabled, most families will go through four predictable stages. These stages are similar to the reactions that an individual would go through if a family member died. The similarity between the birth of a child and the death of a family member is that in both cases there is a loss. When a child with a disability is born, some parents believe it would be easier to lose that child because of death than it is to have a child with a severe disability. With a severely disabled child, their existence and daily needs can be constant reminders of the parents' loss; thus, there is a continuing recurrence of grief. The issue of grief is outlined in greater deal later in the chapter.

All parents will react differently when they are told their children have disabilities. Some parents will live in chronic sorrow; some parents will experience chronic depression; others will reach the final stage of acceptance in a reasonable amount of time. The importance of the reaction cannot be minimized (Alper, Schloss, & Schloss, 1994). Details will be devoted to these reactions later in the chapter.

The phases parents of children with disabilities go through are as follows:

Phase 1: The initial reactions include doubt and disbelief. The parents cannot believe the diagnosis and deny that the diagnose is true.

Phase 2: Awareness develops along with more feelings. Some parents frequently feel guilty. They wonder what they did that caused them to have a child with a disability; they wonder what they could have done differently. During this stage, parents feel anger. They want to know why this happened to them. Often the anger will be directed to other people. If the anger is not controlled, the individual may become depressed. Depression will hinder the parents' ability to manage effectively (Greenbaum, 1994). Also, during this phase, the parents become concerned with their feelings of ambivalence toward their children with disabilities. They feel ashamed because they have negative feelings. They are reluctant to share these feelings with others for fear they will be judged rather than understood. The issue of ambivalence will be addressed in greater details later in the chapter.

Phase 3: During the third phase, the parents do much bargaining, associating a number of "If only I could" statements. This phase
usually lasts for a long time.

Phase 4: In this final phase, parents acknowledge that they have a child
with a disability and are willing to accept him/her. Once this
phase has been successfully met, the parents are open to treatment.

EFFECTS OF FAMILY MEMBERS

Having children with disabilities has an effect on the whole family,
including having an effect on marriages. Some spouses are unable to
tolerate or appreciate the variations in dealing with stress and divorce
may result. In other families, differences are recognized and spouses
turn to others for their needs to be met. In the latter case, the marriage
is likely to stay intact. Siblings are also affected by having a child with
a disability in the family (McLaughlin & Senn, 1994). Children fear
that they can catch what their brother or sister has. They may also
have many questions that need to be answered. Like the parents, the
children need someone they can share their feelings with and get accurate information and answers from. Oftentimes, children are afraid to
ask their questions and pretend everything is in order. It is important
that they be periodically asked if they have any questions. To open dialogue, adults might share some of the questions and feelings they had
about the child with the disability. Given support and encouragement,
most children handle having a sibling with a disability well. They may
benefit from the situation by becoming more sensitive and tolerant of
others, regardless of their differences.

THE PRESENCE OF CHILDREN WITH DISABILITIES

The presence of children with disabilities may have a significant
impact on parents and family members. Marital problems and other
children within the family may be affected. The behavior of children
with disabilities is greatly influenced by the reactions and attitudes of
family members. In essence, what the child with a disability does

affects the total family, and the family responses to the behaviors in turn affect the child. When children with disabilities are reared in home environments which are productive, the children's adjustment in the larger community is usually good. Research has shown that the mother's personality and positive interactions between family members and the child with a disability were more important to the children's well-being than any other practice (Heddel, 1998; Hardman, 1996; Seligman, 1991b).

Sibling Integration

Evidence tends to support that siblings largely adopt their parents' attitudes toward the child with a disability. When negative attitudes and interventions are shown by the parents, siblings usually imitate those behaviors. When nondisabled siblings are made to supervise, care for, protect and defend their disabled peers, negative feelings toward the child with a disability may appear because the time devoted to caring for the child with a disability is depriving the non-disabled sibling of the opportunity to engage in recreational and educational activities.

As indicated, sibling initial reactions will be influenced by the approach utilized by the parents in relating the problem associated with the disability. One important consideration in this respect is the age of the sibling in relation to his ability to grasp the meaning of those factors related to disability, and the capacity to understand the ramifications must be a part of it (Stoneman & Berman, 1993).

If a parent has strong ties with any particular family member, how that member handles the situation will significantly influence what course of action the parent will take, and perhaps even affect the future relationship between them.

The conclusion that can be drawn is that the reactions of the extended family will influence and contribute to the attitudes of the parents both initially and on a continuing basis. What is necessary here is love, understanding, assistance, and encouragement by the family to the parents and ultimately to the child with a disability. With the family's support, the parents will be able to take some comfort in knowing that the family is interested in both them and the child. The parents are looking for strength during this crisis. The family's encouragement and support just may be the catalyst that is needed to assist the parents in adjusting to their problem (Wells, 1997).

The Extended Family

Social factors have a great deal of influence on the adjustment process that parents will make concerning their child with a disability. These factors usually do not bear upon the initial reactions of the parents, but they do affect the later decisions and coping techniques in conjunction with those of the physician, extended family, and religious affiliation.

The parents obviously place great emphasis on what society feels toward their child with a disability, particularly the community segment to which it belongs. Frustrations are increased then when the parents attempt to project what they perceive as society's expectations of them, their abnormal child, and the course of action that should be taken. The integration process of the views of society and the extended family, in relation to the parents, places added strain on the parental perceptions of the child and may, if these views tend to be polarized, create conflicts as to the proper course of action. Parental acceptance or rejection of their child with a disability is thus compounded by the attitudes they hold as well as those attitudes and the value systems expressed by the social environment (Clemens & Brower, 1997).

Parents and siblings should be continuously educated with information relevant to the needs of children with disabilities in the social environments. A first step should be for the community to assess the needs of children with disabilities. A second step should be to develop programs based upon the assessed needs. A third step should be to identify appropriate physical and human resources to augment the program. A final step should be to build with the program an evaluation design to determine the effectiveness of the program.

PERCEPTION OF PARENTS TOWARD DISABILITY

When parents recognize the extent to which their child is disabled, they attempt to seek the cause of the seeming tragedy which has beset them. Two types of motivation seem to underlie this search. The first and more rationale approach is a hope that in discovering the etiology of the disorder, a way might be found that will cure the disability and prevent the occurrence of it in any future children they may have. Additional motivation for the research probably stems from an ardent wish for relief from a heavy burden of responsibility and guilt. One way or another, a great many parents feel that the blame for their child's disability rests with them (Greenbaum, 1994). They may, for example, be concerned because they allowed the baby to roll off the bed or failed to call a physician when he/she was ill. Still others harbor the memory of an unwanted pregnancy, sometimes even of a deliberate attempt to abort the unwanted fetus. In many parents, the most primitive kinds of thinking determine believes about the etiology of the disability. Sometimes the child with a disability becomes the focus of all past wrongdoings of which the parents feel ashamed. Parents who thus blame themselves for their child's disability suffer an additional burden which takes its own trail.

Not only do some parents see a connection between the child with disability and pre- and extramarital transgressions, but unusual intramarital sex practices and intercourse late in pregnancy are felt to give rise to this conflict. The conflict is proliferated when the parent sees the child with a disability as an extension of himself/herself. Ryckman and Henderson (1965) wrote that there are six areas of meaning involved in the parent-child relationship, particularly as it relates to the ego-extension view. Although these views were written over three decades ago, they still have relevance for today's parents. These areas are:

1. The parent considers the child as a physical and psychological extension of himself/herself.
2. The child is a means of vicarious satisfaction to the parents.
3. The parents can derive some measure of immortality through their children.
4. The child is involved in the concept of a personalized love object.
5. There is a parental feeling of worth in responding to the dependency needs of the child.
6. The parents can express negative feelings about the limitations and demands of child rearing.

PARENTAL REACTIONS TOWARD DISABILITIES

Some of the common reactions of parents to their children with disabilities include: (1) not realistically accepting the problem; (2) self-pity; (3) rejection of the problem; (4) guilt, shame, and depression; (5) ambivalence; (6) optimism; and (7) dependency. Many of these reactions may be closely associated with the four phases summarized earlier (Shear & Bauer, 1991; Friend & Rursuck, 1996).

Not Realistically Accepting the Problem

Some parents have developed a common defense against combating anxiety by not realistically accepting the fact that they have a child with a disability. Fathers tend to defend and use other excuses for the child's behavior. Fathers have a difficult time accepting an offspring, which is not normal and an extension of themselves. Initially, most parents of children with disabilities show some type of denial to their children's disabilities. Some parental denial is short-term; others deny their children's disabilities for a prolonged time. There are many factors associated with parental denial of their children with disabilities (Shea & Bauer, 1991; Friend & Bursuck, 1996; Greenbaum, 1994; Hynan, 1996; Hardman, 1996; Alper, 1994). A major factor exists when the parent attempts to hide from him/herself the reality of the fact that his/her child is disabled. This type of behavior impedes constructive and realistic planning for the child. Parents showing this type of behavior are in need of professional assistance in dealing with their problems.

Self-Pity

If parents are not able to develop an objective view towards their children with disabilities, self-pity is likely to develop. Questions frequently posed by parents reflecting self-pity are as follows: What have I done to deserve this? Why me? Have I committed a sin? Why did God do this to me? Without appropriate counseling, parents may become embittered and anti-God.

This type of parental behavior may be attributed to the parent's associating the disability with some past action that he/she has been involved, and that he/she is being punished for by having this child with a disability. Until this self-pity reaction is reversed, little constructive planning can be developed to assist the child, because the parents believe that they are responsible and no amount of intervention will help.

Rejection of the Problem

Rejection of the problem is used as a defense or an excuse to deny the existence of the child. Many parents never particularly accept the child's disability. They may accept the results from the diagnosis but do not accept the prognostic implications. They believe that the disability is not permanent and that a cure will be found; they continually seek and search for professional assistance in eradicating the disability. The parent is not usually cognizant of the child's disability psychological adjustment to the question to make him/her normal. Severe emotional reaction may develop within the child, such as a reduction in his/her self-worth and image.

Guilt and Shame

Most parents of children with disabilities experience some guilt or shame. Guilt refers to the parents' self-condemnation, self-blame, personal disappointment, and a low self-image. These reactions by parents are designed to not recognize or compensate for their feelings of hostility and rejection created by having a child with a disability. Feelings of guilt may result in a lifetime of suffering for the parents. Shame is displayed by parents in several ways. Shame refers to how parents think that other individuals will react and say about having a child with a disability. Many parents become social rejects because they can not successfully cope with having a child with a disability. Some move constantly from neighborhood to neighborhood to avoid establishing direct relationships. Society's reaction to many parents of children with disabilities has forced them to place their children in public and private institutions. As indicated earlier, parents who show guilt and shame reactions will need professional assistance in order to successfully cope with their reactions. Delaying seeking professional assistance will only compound the problem and impede programs for educating the child with a disability.

Ambivalence

Negative reactions may occur when the parents realize that the disabled conditions of their children cannot be reversed, the condition is permanent. Negative reactions vary from wishing that the child was never born or wishing that the child would die unacknowledged, hostility, and rejection. These ambivalent feelings promote quilt reactions which may lead to overprotection and an attempt to deny or compensate for hostile feelings of which the parents is frequently ashamed (Nicholas & Bieber, 1996). Ambivalent feelings toward children with disabilities can result in parents making unrealistic demands upon the children or becoming less tolerant of mistakes made by the child with a disability. As will most reactions, parents will need professional assistance to overcome negative overtones.

Optimism

Many parents are optimistic about their children's disabilities. Many are in constant search, attempting to discover some remedy to eradicate the disability. They take their children from clinic to clinic, from one professional to another. They have not come to grips that the reality of the condition is irreversible. They simply refuse to admit that the child is permanently disabled. They do not believe that diagnostic evaluations are reflective of future (prognostic) evaluations. They believe that one day their child will be normal.

Dependency

A mother and her child with a disability may develop self-perpetuating patterns of mutual dependency. Unknowingly, the mother may develop overdependency in the child with a disability. When a parent devotes a significant part of himself/herself in the care of a child with a disability, a pattern of mutual dependency may exist. Both child and parent become dependent upon each other. Excessive care, supervision, and protection given the child by the parent may promote dependency. If care is not taken, the parent will make serving the child, the center of his/her life. When dependency on the part of both parent and child persist over a period of time, the trend is difficult to reverse. Thus, increasing mutual dependency between mother and child does not promote independence and interferes with constructive programming for the child.

Attempts were made in this section to highlight some of the common reactions that parents show toward their children with disabilities. Many parents will need professional counseling and treatment to overcome many of the negative reactions projected. Chapter 4 has been reserved to outline specific treatment modalities to assist parents in working successfully with their children with disabilities.

SUMMARY

The age of onset, the intensity, financial resources, and complexity of the disability are some factors associated with how parents will react to the disabilities of their children. Most parents react negatively to the birth of a child with a disability. Generally, children with disabilities are perceived as a disappointment and a direct blow to the ego of most parents.

When parents begin to relate their own past to the reason for having children with disabilities, the consequences may be devastating. They may assume that they are being punished for some act in which they committed. These strong emotions impede constructive assistance that they might be normally give to the children and may led to defensive behaviors on part of the parents. These behaviors frequently result in a denial of the existence of a disability and is associated with a term called "defense mechanism."

Parents have few problems maintaining a defensive mechanism approach while the child is young, they simply keep him/her out of the public view. All they have to do during the early years is to convince themselves that there is no disabling condition in their child. As the child becomes older, it becomes extremely difficult to keep the child hidden from the public view, due to school and situations in the community. Strategies which operate during the early years will no longer suffice. Additional strategies must be enacted to maintain the self-deception of the parents. At this point, the parents may need professional services to aid them to cope with the reality of the situation.

The immediate and extended family should be involved in counseling. Families should be provided with current diagnostic information relevant to the child's disability, as well as strategies for dealing with their attitudes and negative feelings. The counselor must deal with the family's multiplicity of fears and anxieties of guilt and shame displayed by many parents. Attempts should be made to reduce the tensions imposed by the child with a disability through providing activities which will increase the tolerance levels and modify the behaviors of the family members. Parents should be provided with information to assist them in understanding that some of their children with disabilities have the possibilities of becoming independent adults. Refer to Chapter 4 for recommended counseling techniques.

REFERENCES

Alper, S. K., Schloss, P. J., & Schloss, C. N. (1994). *Families of students with disabilities.* Boston: Allyn and Bacon.

Clemens-Brower, T. J. (1997). Recruiting parents and the community. *Educational Leadership, 54,* 58-60.

Friend, M., & Bursuck, W. D. (1996). *Including students with special needs.* Boston: Allyn and Bacon.

Lian, M. J., & Aloia, G. (1994). Parental responses, roles, and responsibiliites. In S.K. Alper, P. J. Schloss, & C. N. Schloss (Eds.), *Families of students with disabilities.* Boston: Allyn and Bacon.

Greenbaum. F. K. (1994). Disability really isn't that romantic. *Exceptional Parent, 24*(7), 46-47.

Hardman, M. L., Drew, C. S., & Eagan, W. M. (1996). *Human exceptionality: Social, school, and family.* Boston: Allyn and Bacon.

Harshman, K. 1(1996). Providing resources for parents. *Scholastic Early Childhood Today, 11,* 11.

Heddel, F. (1988). *Children with mental handicaps.* Marlborough, England: Crowood Press.

Hynan, M. T. (1996). Coping with crisis: Confronting the emotions of your fear. *Exceptional Parent, 26,* 64.

McLoughlin, J. A., & Senn, C. (1994). Parental responses, roles, and responsibilities. In S. K. Alper, P. J. Schloss, & C. N. Schloss (Eds.), Families of students with disabilities. Boston: Allyn and Bacon.

Nicholas, K. B., & Bieber, S. L. (1996). Parental abuse versus supportive behaviors and their relation to hostility and aggression in young adults. *Child Abuse and Neglect, 20,* 195-211.

Ryckman, D. B., & Henderson, R. A. (1965). The meaning of a retarded child to his parents: A focus for counselors. *Mental Retardation, 3,* 3.

Seligman, M. (1991a). *The family with a handicapped child* (2nd ed.). Boston: Allyn and Bacon.

Seligman, M. (1991b) Siblings of disabled brothers and sisters. In M. Seligman (Ed.), *The family with a handicapped child* (2nd ed.). Boston: Allyn and Bacon.

Shea, T. M., & Bauer, A. M. (1991). *Parents and teachers of children with exceptionalities: A handbook for collaboration.* Boston: Allyn and Bacon.

Stoneman, Z., & Berman, P. W. (1993). *The effects of mental retardation, disability, and illness on sibling relationships.* Baltimore: Paul H. Brookes.

Wells, K. L. (1997). Professional development for parents. *American School Board, 184,* 38-39.

Chapter 4

COUNSELING PARENTS

INTRODUCTION

Effective counseling techniques can do much to inform parents about the nature, extent, and implications of their children's disabling conditions. Further, many of the emotional strains, unhappiness, and conflicts can be significantly reduced with professional counseling strategies. A first step should be to conduct a needs assessment of the parents. Once conducted, teachers and educators will have factual data for conducting counseling sessions to reduce, minimize, or eradicate problems.

Table 3 was constructed, as a sample, to elicit information from parents relevant to securing information and/or services for their children with disabilities. Once the data in Table 3 are analyzed, responses may be categorized, ranked, or assigned priorities. Informational sessions and conferences may be scheduled to address the problems in a variety of individual and group sessions as reflected in Chapter 10. Parents need detailed information explained in laymen terms, on treatment, intervention, and diagnostic evaluations and etiological information concerning their children. Information relevant to community facilities and services, intervention and treatment, education, related services, and other technical services should be made readily available to them. They should be made aware that their problems are not unique. Many parents have children with disabilities and are seeking way to assist them.

Table 3
NEEDS ASSESSMENT FOR PARENTS OF CHILDREN
WITH DISABILITIES

Name_____ Address_____
Child's Name_____ Teacher_____

Dear Parent:
We need your assistance in order to plan appropriately for your children. Please complete the survey and return to the school as soon as possible. There are no right or wrong answers. We want your opinions on the questions listed.

Please use the following scale in rating your responses relevant to information you need: very much = 5, much = 4, neither = 3, little = 2, none = 1.

1. How can I aid the professionals who work with my child?   1 2 3 4 5

2. Relationships between brothers and sisters.   1 2 3 4 5

3. Ways of explaining disability to children, relatives, and others.   1 2 3 4 5

4. What reward system can I use at home?   1 2 3 4 5

5. How can I judge motor development?   1 2 3 4 5

6. Physical, medical, and social needs of my child.   1 2 3 4 5

7. How is my child evaluated and assessed?   1 2 3 4 5

8. What can I do at home to help my child?   1 2 3 4 5

9. What can I do to help my child's social and physical development? 1 2 3 4 5

10. How infants grow and develop...what's normal?   1 2 3 4 5

11. Parent-professional conferences - How can I contribute?   1 2 3 4 5

12. Arrival of a new child in the family.   1 2 3 4 5

13. How does language develop?   1 2 3 4 5

14. How can feeding and mealtimes be easier?   1 2 3 4 5

15. What services are available in the community to aid my child?   1 2 3 4 5

16. List and rate any other type of information needed.   1 2 3 4 5

TREATMENT

Diagnosis and counseling is one continuing process and should begin simultaneously. It is of prime importance that professional staff members involved in the diagnostic process also be included in counseling. The importance of including parents from the inception to the conclusion of the diagnostic and treatment process cannot be overemphasized. Diagnostic information is of little use to parents unless it can be adjusted to fit into the parents' short-and long-range plans for care of the child. Parents should participate in present and future treatment plans.

Since most parents with children with disabilities suffer from some emotional conflicts, guidance and counseling are deemed important if the child is to be effectively treated. Parents must either change their method of viewing the child or develop ego defense mechanisms such as denial, repression, or a guilt complex. Parents must be helped to deal with their feelings. Unless professional help is given, there exists a great likelihood that the emotional problems of the child will increase. For the best results, both parents should be included in the counseling process (May, 1991; Johnson, 1990; Atkinson & Juntanen; 1994).

Through various guidance and counseling techniques provided by diagnostic clinics, parents can be given professional information about their child. The information, if properly introduced will do much to change the parents' attitudes about their child with a disability. Support and guidance by the clinic's professional staff are of vital importance in teaching the parents effective methods of dealing with the child as well as their own emotional problems. The diversity of parental problems negate that many specialists be involved in the counseling process, depending upon the unique needs of the parents. This involvement can be proliferated by including the parents in the educational process through assisting in school-related projects and guidance for helping their children with school assignments. It is of prime importance that this type of relationship be evident if the child with a disability is to achieve maximum benefit from his/her school program (Casas & Furlong, 1994).

INITIAL IMPACT

Research findings have consistently shown that virtually all parents experience some source of anxiety when a child with a disability is present in the family (Seligman, 1991a). There are special problems faced by parents of children with disabilities. Parents go through many states of adjustment to the fact that their child has a disability. Awareness of the fact confirming the disability may likely cause intense subconscious anger on the part of the parents and development of an innate pattern of parental rejection of the child. Parents often have difficulty coping with these feelings. Even the most mature parents find these subconscious reactions troublesome. While parents differ in their initial reaction, most display helplessness, grief, or guilt in varying degrees. The passage of time has apparently done little to ameliorate this condition.

The initial impact of a child with a disability can be severe and profound, parental coping can be unsuccessful or incomplete, and repeated crises may arise (Bristor, 1994). Many parents may thus suffer from poor mental health. Some of the mechanisms by which this might come about have already been indicated. For most parents of children with disabilities, there is a lack of acceptance of their child. Often the child with a disability is perceived as an intruder, and his/her relationship with his/her parents is frequently fraught with frustration, doubts, fears, guilt, and anger. These barriers combine to prevent the healthy integration of the child with a disability into the family structure (Turnbull & Turnbull, 1993).

In order for most children with disabilities to be successfully integrated into the family structure, parents will need some form of counseling. Counseling will enable the parent to view the child in a different perspective. Unless professional help is given, there exists a great likelihood that the emotional problems of both child and parents will increase. Professional personnel can serve a valuable function in showing parents how to deal effectively with their children with disabilities. It should be noted that all professionals are not trained to counsel parents of children with disabilities; however, they can serve as agents in the referring process.

COUNSELING TECHNIQUES

Theoretically, the professional therapist or counselor is the ideal person to counsel parents. The psychological problems, although different in focus, should be amendable to traditional therapeutic techniques. However, there are some who are hindered by their traditional approach to therapeutic problems. Many times, parents require assistance immediately and a flexible approach involving prolonged contact may not be necessary. Research findings have indicated that short-term therapy for crisis intervention can produce effective results. The psychological state of the parents, age, number of children, and sex of the child with a disability are some of the factors that will determine the type and degree of counseling. Therefore, the counselor/therapist should be highly trained and competent in his/her field in order that he/she might appropriately guide the parent (Bradley, Knoll, & Agosta, 1992).

Counseling for parents of children with disabilities is not designed to eradicate all of the problems that parents encounter with their children, rather; it is to provide strategies for the parents to deal more effectively with problems related by their children with disabilities.

ROLES OF PROFESSIONALS

Based upon the nature and extent of the disability, many parents may be counseled by professionals from several disciplines. Counselors should be trained to be active listeners. They must give the parents sufficient time to present their cases. Parents should be encouraged to discuss their problems and identify areas in which they need assistance, the type of services their children have had, and the expectations they have for their children's future (Brandt, 1998; Friend & Bursuck, 1996).

As indicated, many parents of children with disabilities do not understand the professional jargon used by most professionals. Many parents do not understand the language used by many professionals and are frightened by their terminologies. Effective counseling techniques and strategies should include using the vocabulary and communication level of the parents. Professionals should adapt and modify their approaches based upon the parents' level of understanding. Parents should be assured that their children will be treated as individuals, not cases or statistics.

Parents also need counseling in accepting their children's disabilities. Counselors should provide strategies to the shame and guilt shown by many parents. Counselors and educators should be aware of the intense social pressure experienced by these parents. Some parents may become defensive and hostile due to social pressures as well as unsympathetic counselors. Counselors and educators should be patient, show understanding, acceptance, and empathy when counseling parents. By using this approach, counselors can reinforce certain behaviors of parents and reject others without forming judgmental bias or condemning relevant parental statements concerning their disabled children (Muir-Hutchinson, 1987; Turnbull & Turnbull, 1990; Gartner & Lopsky, 1991; Bradley & Knoll, 1992; Turnbull & Turnbull, 1993).

THE ROLE OF EDUCATION AND GUIDANCE

The major role of educators in the treatment and guidance of parents of children with disabilities is to provide correct knowledge and information. When in doubt, educators should refer parents to appropriate professionals. The educator's role is to not to counsel parents but merely to direct and recommend them to professionals.

Professionals must establish the emotional levels of parents before effective treatment can be initiated. Some parents have a high level of acceptance; other have a low acceptance level. Professionals must assess the level of acceptance and provide appropriate intervention and treatment (Shea & Bauer, 1991; Dettmer, 1993).

ETIOLOGY OF THE DISABILITY

As indicated throughout this chapter, parents need to be fully apprised of the etiology and the extent of the disabilities of their children. They also need to know the extent and depth of the disabilities, the amount of sensory acuity in tact, the nature and types of treatment needed, prognostic information, and the availability of community resources. Parental understanding of the etiology of their children's disabilities provides them with a realistic view of the limitations and assets of the children. This understanding on the part of the parent can lead to realistic intervention and planning (Amlund & Kardash, 1994; Blacher, 1984; Turnbull & Turnbull, 1993).

COUNSELING FAMILIES

It has been projected throughout this chapter that the total family must be involved in the counseling process if it is to be successful. Skilled professionals certified in their respective disciplines should conduct the counseling. Educators who are not certified in counseling should not attempt to conduct sessions. The educator or teacher's role should be to provide support to the family. Coleman (1986) suggested that some parental problems are beyond the teacher's competencies and should be referred to appropriate professionals. He listed the following conditions:

1. Parents experience a period of unusual financial difficulty, marital discord, or emotional upheaval.
2. Parents routinely express feelings of helplessness or depression.
3. Parents feel unable to control their child.
4. Parents report that the child is habitually in trouble with juvenile authorities.
5. Parents chronically appear to be under a high level of stress.
6. Parents impose on the teacher's time at home or school with their personal problems.

Although Coleman made the aforementioned conditions in 1986, they still have relevance for today. Parents have varying counseling needs. Some will be defensive, and others will be resistant to treatment because of previous treatment. Counseling techniques are designed to reduce and minimize these types of behaviors.

The total family should be involved in any treatment. Family therapy should be continued throughout the lifetime of the child; the approach should be aware of community resources and services in the community so that they might make appropriate referrals. The end results of counseling should be to assist the family to set realistic goals for their children with disabilities, as to set realistic and coordinated goals for them with their own expectations.

EMOTIONAL NEEDS OF THE PARENTS

As discussed in previous paragraphs, parents display a wide range of emotional problems. The emotional reactions of parents should be fully assessed before treatment or intervention is attempted. Frequently, parents are not aware of the consequences of their emotional reactions on the child, the school, and the family. Professionals should assist parents to understand the nature, cause, and result of their psychological defense and indicate ways how this defense can be minimized. The parents should be made to understand that they are not alone, but many other parents have similar problems. Parents should be encouraged to react and participate in parent groups involved with their children with disabilities. Parents sharing similar problems can do much to elevate individual problems of parents (Shea & Bauer, 1991).

Parental problems may be addressed individually or in groups. The therapist must assess the best approach for the parent. This research believes that some parents might initially be treated individually, but the long-range plan should be to involve the parents in group activities where common views can be shared and discussed. This view is supported by a preponderance of research. Group activities have proven to be highly effective for educative and guidance sessions. Additionally, group activities may serve as a method where valuable procedural methods may be shared by each parent. They enable parents who have similar problems (Atkinson & Juntunen, 1994; Bradley & Knoll, 1992; Muir-Hutchinson, 1987; Coleman, 1986; Shea & Bauer, 1991).

GROUP AND INDIVIDUAL PSYCHOTHERAPY

Some parents' emotional problems are so severe that they may require group or individual psychotherapy to deal with their emotional problems (Shea & Bauer; 1991; Blacher, 1984; Coleman, 1986). The more negative and withdrawn the parent is the more likely he/she is to react in a negative way to the additional problems projected by the child with a disability. Parents who have these severe emotional reactions cannot be successfully treated through education and counseling alone. They are in need of specific treatment designed to reduce or minimize the emotional problems. Some parents may profit significantly from group psychotherapy, whereas others will need individual psychotherapy. Once assessed by the therapist, the major type of psychotherapy will depend upon the emotional problems of the parent as well as his/her personality makeup. Treatment is designed to assist the parents to achieve a satisfactory level of functioning and adjustment, by learning to cope and to tolerate his/her symptoms. Detailed types of psychotherapy are beyond the scope of this text. The readers are referred to any basic text on psychotherapy techniques and strategies.

SUMMARY

The goals of counseling parents of children with disabilities are basically those techniques used to counsel any group. There are no separate groups of counseling techniques used to counsel parents of children with disabilities. Some modifications or adaptations of the methods employed may differ, but the basic counseling techniques and principles remain the same. Parents of children with disabilities need information relevant to their children's intellectual, social/emotional, and physical deficits and how these deficits have impacted upon their disabilities. They need information relevant to community agencies and facilities which may provide care and treatment to their children, interpreting diagnostic information and terminology, dealing with accepting their children's disabilities, and strategies for involving the immediate and extended family in the counseling process. Skilled and competent counselors are needed to provide professional services to parents of children with disabilities.

Counselors or therapists have a wide variety of strategies and techniques to employ to assist parents in dealing effectively with their children with disabilities. Groups and individual techniques may be used, based upon the assessed needs of the parents, such as group and individual psychotherapy. Therapists are trained to determine the nature and extent of the psychotherapy to be induced, which is designed to assist both the child and the parents to successfully cope with problems imposed by the disabilities

REFERENCES

Amlund, J. T., & Kardash, C. M. (1994). In S. K. Alper, P. J. Schloss, & C. N. Schloss (Eds.), *Families of students with disabilities*. Boston: Allyn and Bacon.

Atkinson, D. R., & Juntunen, C. L. (1994). School counselors and school psychologists as school-home-community liaisons in ethnically diverse schools. In P. Pederson & J. C. Carey (Eds.), *Multi-cultural counseling in schools: A practical handbook*. Boston: Allyn and Bacon.

Blacker, J. (1984). Sequential stages of parental adjustment to the birth of a child with handicaps: Fact or artifact? *Mental Retardation, 22*(2), 55-68.

Bradley, V. J., Knoll, J., & Agosta, J. M. (1992). *Emerging issues in family support*. Washington, DC: The American Association on Mental Retardation.

Brandt, R. (1998). Listen first. *Educational Leadership, 55*(8), 25-30.

Bristor, M. W. (1984). The birth of a handicapped child: A holistic model for grieving. *Family Relations, 33*, 25-32.

Casas, M., & Furlong, M. J. (1994). School counselors as advocates for increased Hispanic parent participation in schools. In P. Pederson, & J. C. Carey (Eds.). *Multi-cultural counseling in schools: A practical handbook*. Boston: Allyn and Bacon.

Coleman, M. C. (1986). *Behavior disorders: Theory and practice*. Englewood Cliffs, NJ: Prentice-Hall.

Dettmer, P., Thurston, L. P., & Dyck, N. (1993). *Consultation, collaboration, and teamwork for students with special needs*. Boston,: Allyn and Bacon.

Friend, M., & Bursuck, W. (1996). *Including students with special needs: A practical guide for classroom teachers*. Boston: Allyn and Bacon.

Gartner, A., Lipsky, D. K., & Turnbull, A. P. (1991). *Supporting families with a child with disabilities*. Baltimore: Paul H. Brookes.

Johnson, N. (1990). Evolving attitudes about family support. *Family Support Bulletin*, 12-13

May, J. (1991). Commentary: What about fathers? *Family Support Bulletin*, 19.

Muir-Hutchinson, L. (1987). Working with professionals. *Exceptional Parent, 17*(5), 8-10.

Seligman, M. (1991a). The family with a handicapped child (2 nd ed.). Boston: Allyn and Bacon.

Shea, T. M., & Bauer, A. M. (1991). Parents and teachers of children with exceptionalities: A handbook for collaboration. Boston: Allyn and Bacon.

Turnbull, A. P., & Turnbull, H.R. (1990). *Families, professionals, and exceptionality* (2nd ed.). Columbus, OH: Merrill.

Turnbull, A. P., & Turnbull, H. R. (1993). Participating research on cognitive coping: From concepts to research planning. In A. P. Turnbull , J. M. Patterson, S. K. Behr, D. L. Murphy, D. L. Marquis, & M. J. Blue-Banning (Eds.), *Cognitive coping, families, and disabilities*. Baltimore: Paul H. Brookes.

Chapter 5

IMPACT OF FEDERAL LEGISLATION ON PARENTAL INVOLVEMENT

INTRODUCTION

Federal and state legislation were necessary to guarantee parent equal education opportunities for their children with disabilities. Historically, parents and associations involved with disabled individuals were responsible for state and federal legislation as well as court cases involving the education of their children. Their actions and involvement made a significant impact in practices and procedures for educating children with disabilities (Hardman, Drew, Egan, & Wolf, 1992).

Two of the most importance court cases affecting the education of children with disabilities are:

1. Pennsylvania Association for Retarded Children v. the Commonwealth of Pennsylvania in 1972.
2. Mills v. Washington, D.C. Board of Education.

Both cases dealt with the right of disabled children to full access to a free and appropriate education. Parents and the Association for Retarded Citizens were responsible for the success in these course cases. Success of the court cases were responsible for passage of several state and federal legislation. Those state and federal legislation outlined specific ways for parental involvement in the education of their children.

Several federal legislation were enacted based upon the success of the court cases. Public Law 93-112, Section 504 (The Rehabilitation Act of 1973), established equal rights for all individuals with disabilities. Section 501 of the same act forbids federal departments and agencies from discrimination in employment based upon handicapping conditions. Section 502 sets standards for eliminating architectural, transportation, and attitudinal barriers confronting handicapped individuals. Section 503 mandated that federal contractors and subcontractors refrain from discriminating against handicapped individuals in employment and promotion practices (Shea & Bauer, 1991; National Council on Disability, 1995).

Public Law 93-380 is designed to protect the educational rights legislated in Public Law 93-112. The major components involve: (1) expenditure of federal money to implement the law; (2) development of a state plan to ensure procedural safeguards for the identification, evaluation, and educational placement of handicapped children; (3) placement of exceptional children in the least restrictive educational setting capable on meeting their needs; (4) use of a parent surrogate as an advocate when the parent cannot be located.

The Buckley Amendment to Public Law 93-380 was legislated to protect the rights and privacy of students and parents. It mandated that schools cannot release information on a child without parental consent. The amendment also gave parents the right to examine school records and to challenge irrelevant information (U.S. Department of Education, 1995).

The federal laws laid the framework for the establishment of national policy, which set standards regulating federal, state, and local policies governing educational services and programs for handicapped children and their parents. Public Law 94-142 combined and made these policies operational on the national level, mandating a free, appropriate public education for all handicapped children (Turnbull & Turnbull, 1996).

PUBLIC LAW 94-142

Public Law 94-142 and other federal legislation have mandated that parents be involved in planning education experiences of their children with disabilities. Individual Education Plan (IEP), which is part of P.L. 94-142 and P.L. 105-17, mandated parental involvement, from initial identification to placement of children with disabilities into educational settings. (Refer to Appendix B for a summary of P.L. 105-17.)

The emphasis on P.L. 94-142 and subsequent revisions are the requirements that parental consent be obtained for any decisions made in the IEP process and that parents always be informed of any steps taken in the IEP process, whether they concern prereferral, referral, evaluation, service, treatment, progress, annual review, and modifications of the IEP. Parental consent is the voluntary agreement of the parent or guardian after being apprised of all information in a comprehensive form. Parent awareness and approval are essential.

PARENT PARTICIPATION IN ELIGIBILITY PLACEMENT AND ASSESSMENT DECISIONS

Under the old IDEA, parent participation was not required for making decisions regarding a student's eligibility for special education and related services. Under the new legislation, parents are specifically included as members of the group making the eligibility decision. (Refer to Appendix C for additional details.)

Parent participation in placement decisions is similarly required. Under the old legislation, parent involvement in deciding the placement of their child was not required. The new IDEA clarified the parents' right to be involved in such decisions. (Refer to Appendix D for additional readings.)

IEP INVOLVEMENT

According to Hardman, Drew, and Egan (1993), IDEA mandated the following rights for parents.

1. To consent in writing before the child is initially evaluated.
2. To consent in writing before the child is initially placed in a special education program.
3. To request an independent education evaluation if the parent feels the school's evaluation is inappropriate.
4. To request an evaluation at public expense if a due process hearing finds that the public agency's evaluation was inappropriate.
5. To participate on the committee that considers the evaluation, placement, and programming of the child.

6. To inspect and review educational records and challenge information believed to be inaccurate, misleading, or in violation of the privacy or other rights of the child.
7. To request a copy of information from the child's education record.
8. To request a hearing concerning the school's proposal or refusal to initiate or change the identification, evaluation, or placement of the child or the provision of a free, appropriate public education

The schools have not done an effective job in meeting the federal mandates. Educators must think of an experiment with innovative ways of involving parents in the schools. Over the last several decades, the schools have had a difficult time in establishing effective partnerships with parents. Much of the fragmentation has occurred because of noninvolvement, hostility, or parental indifference towards the schools (Harry & McLaughlin, 1995).

If IEP team members feel that they do not have enough information to answer the above questions, then tests and other evaluative procedures would be conducted in order to gather specific information needed. If, however, they feel that sufficient data exist to address these questions, then the school system is not required to reevaluate the child. Parents must be notified of that determination, as well as their right to request that their child be reevaluated anyway. If parents request such a reevaluation, the school must conduct it. An important change in the law requires that parents give their consent before any reevaluation of the child may be conducted. If parents fail to respond to the school's request for consent, however, the school may under certain conditions proceed without it.

In order to ensure that the rights and privacy of parents and their children with disabilities are protected, federal regulations directed all state and local school districts to develop procedural safeguards for parents and their children. Due to changes in the various amendments to federal legislation, safeguard procedures have been slightly modified to meet the letter of the law. As a result, procedural safeguards are reported for both the old and new IDEA.

PROCEDURAL SAFEGUARDS: OLD LAW

Public Law 94-142 and its amendments give parents the right to "Procedural Safeguards" and the right to "Due Process" instituted for them. 1(Refer to Appendix E for a parent due process checklist.) These procedural safeguards address the following areas:

A. Records

1. Parents have the right to examine all educational records concerning their children. These records contain the following kinds of information:

   a. Information about identification and evaluation of their children.

   b. Information about the educational placement of their children.

   c. Other information about providing a free, appropriate public education.

2. Both the state and local education agency must maintain a list of the types and location of information collected, maintained, and used, and must make this list available to parents, upon request.

3. An additional record must be kept of all personnel who have had access to the information collected. This record must include the name of the individual, the date, and the purpose for which the information was sought.

4. Any personally identifiable data, information, or records collected by either the SEA or the LEA must be kept confidential.

5. Both the SEA and the LEA have the right to charge a fee for copies made of this information, providing that the charge is reasonable and does not prevent the exercise of rights by any party. No fee can be charged for search or retrieval of any information.

6. At any point, parents may request an amendment to the informational record kept on their child. The education agency must respond within a reasonable time to the request for an amendment. If the agency chooses not to make the amendment, they must inform the parents of their right to a hearing to challenge the record. If at the hearing, a decision is made to amend the record, the LEA must inform the parents in writing about the decision. If the decision is not to amend the educational record, parents still have the right to place an amending statement in the record. This statement will be maintained as though it was part of the original record.

7. All agencies must obtain written parental consent before any identifiable information is disclosed to anyone other than authorized personnel, or before that information is used for any purpose not required by law. Should there be a refusal of parent consent, the information cannot be disclosed.

8. Before any information is destroyed, a reasonable effort must be made to notify parents of their right to a copy.

9. At the parents' request, the SEA and LEA must destroy any personally identifiable data after it is no longer needed. A permanent record may be maintained which can only include the following information: (a) name, (b) address, (c) phone numbers, (d) grades, (e) attendance record, (f) classes attended, (g) grade level completed, and (h) the year completed.

B. Assessments

Another area in which procedural safeguards must be maintained concerns the evaluation of children.

1. All children receiving special education services must have an educational evaluation.

2. Parents or guardians must give their written permission before their child receives an educational evaluation.

3. No single evaluation procedure can be the sole criteria for making program and/or placement decisions. Information from other sources must be considered, including information concerning physical condition, educational history, and adaptive behavior in home and school.

4. Assessment practices must not be racially or culturally discriminatory.

5. If the parents feel that their child has not had access to a fair assessment, the parents are entitled to obtain an independent evaluation at public expense. However, the LEA may initiate a hearing to show that its assessment is appropriate. If the final decision at the hearing is that the LEA assessment is appropriate, the parents still have the right to an independent evaluation, but not at public expense. Parents should exercise caution regarding independent evaluations because they can be very costly and this expense becomes the parents' responsibility if the decision at the hearing is that the LEA assessment was appropriate.

6. All rights which parents have must be available to the student when he/she reaches the age of 18.

C. Program Planning

1. Parents have a right to know about their children's educational program. That is, parents must be notified in writing before there are any changes or attempts to change their children's educational identification, evaluation, or educational placement. Parents

must be notified in writing that an Admission, Review, and Dismissal Committee (ARD Committee) is meeting to discuss their child and that they may attend the ARD meeting. The parents must be notified early enough so that they can arrange to attend, and the meeting must be held at a time and place that is convenient for the parents. The parents may bring whomever they wish to the meeting. Their notice must tell them:

a. The purpose of the meeting.
b. The time and location of the meeting.
c. Who will be attending.

2. The individualized educational program (IEP) is a written account of the educational programs and services, which the school is going to implement for the child. If the parents agree to the individualized educational program, the parents are required to sign the IEP. The school then must provide those services which are identified in the IEP. If the parent asks for a copy of the IEP, the school is required to send them one.

3. Any information which the parent receives must be in the primary language or primary model of communication (for example, sign language). The IEP law requires that ARD Committee meetings and IEP meetings be held within a certain period of time, and that those programs and services identified on the IEP begin with certain. IEP timelines–from initiation to annual review.

D.Hearings

If for any reason parents or guardians feel that their child is not being provided a free, appropriate public education, or if there is any disagreement between the parents and the local education agency regarding identification, evaluation, or educational placement, the parents or guardians have the right to a "due process hearing."

Due process simply stated means fair procedure. Under the law, schools must use fair procedures in all matters regarding parents and students. Due process is one of the most important constitutional rights of parents and students. A due process checklist appears in Appendix E.

The rights specified will assist parents in staying on top of decisions about their children. While a due process hearing is their right, it can be an exhausting process. Before proceeding on this route, parents should have tried to resolve differences through every other means–by being as well-prepared and persuasive as possible with teachers, specialists, and administrators. If conflicting points of view cannot be resolved except by a due process hearing, parents should prepare their cases as thoroughly as possible. Parents may wish to receive advice or other assistance from anyone of a number of sources including the state Department of Education, recognized associations representing disabled people, established advocacy groups, or they may want legal consultation. The school system must advise parents of sources of free or low-cost legal aid.

The following points ensure the implementation of due process procedures for everyone:

- The law states that local hearing is to be commenced and completed as quickly as possible, and in most states, means no later than 45 days after their is receipt of a written request for a hearing.
- Parents have the right to be notified in writing about the decision reached as a result of the local hearing. This written decision must be rendered within 5 days of the hearing and written notification of this decision must be made to the parents within 5 days. If parents are dissatisfied with the decision, they may appeal the decision within 30 days to the state Department of Education for a hearing before a three member board of independent hearing officers which will conduct an impartial review within 30 days of receipt of a written appeal and render an independent decision. These timelines operate in most states.
- Should the decision by the state Hearing Review Board not be agreeable to the parents, they have the right to take civil action in the state or United States District Court, or any one of the three Common Law Courts of the Supreme Bench.
- The hearing shall be impartial. That is, it must be conducted by someone not employed by the agency responsible for the child's education or care. For example, any local education agency employee may not serve or be considered an impartial hearing officer.
- Parents or guardians have the right to legal advice or counsel and to be accompanied by counsel at this hearing. Parents may also be accompanied by individuals who have special knowledge or training with respect to the problems of their child.
- Parents, either themselves or through their counsel, have the right to present evidence and to question witnesses. They also have the

right to compel the attendance of any witnesses with special knowledge or training about the problem of their child.

- Both parties to the hearing have the right to prohibit the introduction of any evidence which has not been disclosed to them at least five days prior to the hearing.
- When it seems appropriate, the child himself/herself has the right to be present.
- When the parents or guardians wish, the hearing may be open to the public.
- Parents have a right to a written or electronic verbatim record of the hearing at reasonable cost.

One question often raised is "What happens to the children while these decisions are pending?" According to the law, the children have the right to stay in the educational program where they were originally placed before any action began. If the parents or guardians of the children are applying for initial admission to a public school program, the children may be placed in that program until all the proceedings have been completed, if the parents or guardians agree to that placement. During any of these proceedings, the educational program which is agreed upon must be provided at no cost to the parents/guardians. As with the IEP, the law requires a certain time within which these hearing procedures must take place. (See Appendix F for strategies to employ when a child's behavior is a manifestation of his/her disability.)

NEW SAFEGUARD PROCEDURES

The new law (IDEA) added specific requirements regarding safeguard procedures for parents. A copy of the procedural safeguards available to the parents of a child with a disability shall be given to the parents, at a minimum:

- upon initial evaluation;
- upon each notification of an individualized education program meeting and upon re-evaluation of the child;
- upon registration of a complaint under subsection (b) (6);
- contents–The procedural safeguards notice shall include a full explanation of the procedural safeguards, written in the native language of the parents,

unless it clearly is not feasible to do so, and written in an easily understandable manner, available under this section and under regulations promulgated by the Secretary relating to:

- independent educational evaluation;
- prior written notice;
- parental consent;
- access to educational records;
- opportunity to present complaints;
- the child's placement during pendency of due process proceedings;
- procedures for students who are subject to placement in an interim alternative educational setting;
- requirements for unilateral placement by parents of children in private schools at public expense;
- mediation;
- due process hearings, including requirements for disclosure of evaluation results and recommendations;
- State-level appeals (if applicable in that State);
- civil actions; and
- attorney's fees.

A. If the child's parent/guardian disagrees with a determination that the child's behavior was not a manifestation of the child's disability or with any decision regarding placement, the parent/guardian may request a hearing. The State or local educational agency shall arrange for an expedited hearing in any case described in this subsection when requested by a parent/guardian:

- In reviewing a decision with respect to the manifestation determination, the hearing officer shall determine whether the public agency has demonstrated that the child's behavior was not a manifestation of such child's disability consistent with the requirements of paragraph (4) (C).
- In reviewing a decision under paragraph (1) (A) (ii) to place the child in an interim alternative educational setting, the hearing officer shall apply the standards set out in paragraph (2).

Placement during appeals. When a parent requests a hearing regarding a disciplinary action described in paragraph (1) (A) (ii) or paragraph (2) to challenge the interim alternative educational setting or the manifestation determination, the child shall remain in the interim alternative educational setting pending the decision of the hearing officer until the expiration of the time period provided for in paragraph (1) (A) (ii) or paragraph (2), whichever occurs first, unless the parent/guardian and the state or local educational agency agree otherwise.

B. Current placement. If a child is placed in an interim alternative educational setting pursuant to paragraph (1) (A) (ii) or paragraph (2) and school personnel propose to change the child's placement after expiration of the interim alternative placement, during the pendency of any proceeding to challenge the proposed change in placement, the child shall remain in the current placement (the child's placement prior to the interim alternative educational setting), except as provided in subparagraph (c).

C. Expedited hearing. If school personnel maintain that it is dangerous for the child to be in the current placement (placement prior to removal to the interim alternative education setting) during the pendency of the due process proceedings, the local educational agency may request an expedited hearing. In determining when whether the child may be placed in another appropriate placement ordered by the hearing officer.

The old IDEA was addressed earlier in the chapter. The new IDEA increased parental participation in eligibility decisions, placement, prior written notices before decisions are made, and written notices to parents must be in their native language (The National Information Center for Children and Youth with Disabilities, 1998; U. S. Department of Education, Individuals with Disability Education Act Amendments of 1997).

In essence, the purpose of safeguards and the due process requirements are to ensure as much as possible that all parents/guardians be an essential part of planning education and services for their children with disabilities. In the event that parents/guardians elect to participate in the planning process, the school should have records to show that attempts were made to involve them. In most school districts, parental involvement is sought in four components:

1. At the time of referral for special education: Parental notification of the meeting is usually required before any type of assessment is conducted.
2. At planning conferences: Parental involvement, through their consent for approving services for their children with disabilities, is expected. If parental consent is not given because they believe the services are not appropriate, due process procedures may be implemented.
3. In finalizing the educational program: Parental endorsement is needed to approve any significant changes in the student's program or related services.
4. In phasing out special education or related services: Parental permission is needed to modify or cancel any special education service.

If the parent is dissatisfied with the school district's plans or the related services being provided, the parent may request an impartial due process hearing. At such a hearing, the parents and school officials may be represented by legal counsel. When a request for a due process hearing is made, an impartial hearing officer is appointed by the state education agency, and a formal hearing is held at which both sides present evidence and a verbatim transcript of the proceedings is kept. The impartial hearing officer evaluates the evidence and issues a ruling. If the parties do not wish to abide by the ruling, a state-level hearing may be requested. The impartial hearing officer makes a recommendation to the chief state school officer, who issues a ruling that is binding on all parties involved. The only recourse available to a parent or a school district beyond the state-level hearing is to take the matter to court. The process outlined above is accurate with minor variations for nearly all of the fifty states.

The due process procedure makes no presumptions of who is right or wrong in a conflict. The impartial hearing officer's role is to hear both sides and render a decision. Although the major purpose of the due process is to protect the rights of children and their parents, frequently, judgments and decisions are made not supporting the parents. The impartial process is far from perfect for the following reasons:

1. The process assumes that the impartial Hearing Officer is trained and competent in special education matters and understands the process.
2. Many parents are not familiar with the process and do not know procedural safeguards mandated by law.
3. Many parents do not want to get involve in a long and time-consuming process to prepare for a hearing.
4. Parents who receive a favorable ruling feel that they have created negative feelings in the school district by having their cases supported.

The impartial hearing process is not perfect, but it is a first step in the due process for parents and it reduces the number of special education cases going to court. Another approach in reducing the number of court cases is to train and inform parents about special education by developing partnerships between professionals and families.

DEVELOPING A PARTNERSHIP BETWEEN FAMILIES AND PROFESSIONALS

During the past 25 years, a significant shift in philosophy has occurred regarding the relationship between families of children with disabilities and professionals that serve them (Winton, 1994; Turnbull

& Turnbull, 1996). Unlike the past, today's professionals consider the family as a unit instead of solely focusing on the mother-child dyad; they also understand there are family issues beyond those related to the child that must be addressed to effectively serve children with disabilities. Now professionals not only consider the needs of the family but also its strengths when developing educational programs that meet the child's needs. This philosophical shift has influenced the development of special education legislation and the relationship between families and professionals.

Involvement of families in decisions about their child's education is a central component of family-school collaboration (Turnbull & Turnbull, 1996), and the role that families can have in the education of their child with disabilities has evolved since the passage of P.L. 94-142. Families of school-aged children served through the IDEA, Part B have tended to be less involved in decisions than those of infants and toddlers served under Part H. Although families of school-aged children served under Part B are entitled to participate in their child's IEP meeting, many do not. A recent longitudinal study conducted in a large urban and primarily minority school district found that parent attendance at IEP meetings decreased over a three-year period (Harry, Allen, & McLaughlin, 1995). In contrast, family participation is at the core of the Part H program. This emphasis is evident in many ways. One example is the importance given to families at the individualized family service plan (IFSP) meeting for infants and toddlers with disabilities. During these meetings, families are an integral part of the process of designing the IFSP. This perspective is, in part, an outgrowth of the systems perspective of human development which emphasizes that children with disabilities do not exist in a vacuum. To comprehend the impact of the disability, one must gain an understanding of the context of children's lives (Turnbull, Turnbull, & Shankon, 1995).

This module describes some of the changes that have occurred in parent-professional partnerships. It addresses a systems perspective of human development. This issue has been summarized in great detail in Chapter 1. The remaining sections discuss the type of partnerships that have developed as a result of IDEA.

Family Collaboration in IDEA, Part H

In 1986, Part A of IDEA stipulated that a family-centered approach be used in serving eligible children from birth to age three. Also, a commitment to the parent-professional partnership is embedded throughout the Part A regulations. Part A established the individualized family service plan (IFSP) and required that professionals collaborate with families when developing a plan for the child, consider the entire family when deciding on services, and choose services that strengthen families. As part of these requirements, the IFSP documents the family's resources, priorities, and concerns related to the development of the child (34 CFR 303.344(b)).

In an attempt to measure the degree to which early intervention services are being implemented in a family-centered manner, McBride, Brotherson, Joanning, Whiddon, and Demmitt (1993) conducted semi-structured interviews with 15 families receiving early intervention services and with 14 professionals. A major finding of the study was that over time, a shift toward family-centered practices had occurred. All of the families stated that professionals showed concern for the family, not just the child with disabilities. Also, the professionals articulated that implementing the IFSP requirements changed their professional practice orientation from child-focused to family-focused. However, when describing their practice, five of the 14 professionals discussed goals that were still based on a child-focused orientation. The study also examined the families' role in the decision-making process. Four families deferred decision-making to the professionals, and three families chose to share the role. Ten families believed they could learn the most about their child by observing the professional and answering questions, and more than half the families described their role in the decision-making process as having the final veto power. Finally, many of the families stated that their emotional well-being had improved through contact with professionals who showed concern for their emotional needs and with other parents who were in a similar situation.

Another study (Bailey, Palsha, & Simeonsson, 1991) found that professionals were concerned about their changing roles. Results of a survey of 142 professionals working in early intervention programs in two states showed that professionals perceived a moderate level of competence in their ability to work with parents and a higher level of competence working with children. However, as a group, they considered their role of working with families as important. Their primary concerns were how family-centered practices would affect them personally and whether they had the skills to engage in such practices. This study also suggests that the level and type of training given to professionals can significantly influence parent-professional relationships.

Family Collaboration in IDEA, Part B

The relationship between parents and professionals may change when children with disabilities turn three and begin preschool. For most families, the setting in which services take place changes from the home to the school. Regularly scheduled private home visits between families and professionals end. Children are served within a group setting, and parents may be invited into the child's classroom. They may take on the role of parent helper or observer. Also, school districts may transition to an IEP to develop goals and objectives for the child instead of using an IFSP to address the needs of the child and the resources, priorities, and concerns of the family. Therefore, the goals and objectives tend to become more child-centered than family-centered.

Typically, parents of children in primary and secondary special education programs are given less support and have less input into their child's education than parents of children from birth through age five (Winton, 1994). However, there are both informal and formal ways (e.g., IEP and individualized transition plan (ITP) meetings) to encourage parent involvement and thereby increase collaboration. Informal involvement includes the many opportunities for parent-teacher communication. This can include written notes between school and home, parent involvement in the classroom and extracurricular activities, telephone contact, technology options such as the Internet, and conferences (Turnbull & Turnbull, 1996). Increasing this communication to include the accomplishments of the child as well as the child's needs is an important part of developing collaboration.

OSEP recognizes the importance of the role that families need to play and is taking steps to promote an increase in the participation of families served through IDEA, Part B and Part H. A four-step plan to strengthen the working relationship between families and schools has been proposed. It includes: "(1) increasing involvement of families in decision-making, (2) improving information available to families, (3) linking families to other resources and supports in the community, and (4) reducing adversarial dispute resolution by using mediation" (U.S. Department of Education, 1995).

The Challenge of Transition

There are several important factors to consider when providing services to families. One, as mentioned earlier, is to have an understanding of the family's perspective in order to develop a collaborative relationship between families and professionals. Another is the understanding that one of the most important factors in families' lives is the attainment of certain milestones. Often these life milestones are used to determine when services should be given. These milestones or transitions that occur during one's lifetime can be traced in a variety of ways. Two of the possibilities, as described by Mallory (1996), are developmental transitions and institutional transitions. Developmental transitions are associated with the maturational milestones an individual reaches in life, such as learning to walk or talk during the first years of life, reaching puberty, childbearing, and having children leave home. Institutional transitions mark the changes of moving from one institutional setting to another. They include events such as entering daycare; elementary, middle, or high school; college or military service; and the workforce (Morningstar & Turnbull, 1995).

The timing of when to administer services can be as influential on the family as the services themselves. Social policies have emphasized institutional transitions, which are often independent from the developmental transitions. This can have negative effects on individuals with disabilities and their families. For example, the individual experiencing the transition may lose his or her locus of control and transition from setting to setting, based on institutional transitions that are dictated by social policies such as laws and regulations. The likelihood of this happening increases if the individual has a disability and an assumption is made that the individual is less capable of making his or her own decisions (Mallory, 1996). However, if there is an open dialogue and a partnership between families and professionals, the likelihood of the family or individual losing control is reduced.

Two institutional transitions in special education are the transition from IDEA, Part H, to IDEA, Part B, at age three and the transition from school to postschool activities. These are formal opportunities for parent-professional collaboration. The Part B regulations contain provisions for a smooth transition that take place while the individual is served through Part B or ready to exit any or all Part B services (34 CFR 300.344(c) and 300.346(b)). The Part B regulations stress parent participation during IEP meetings as well as during transition periods (34 CFR 300.345). Fostering positive interactions during these meetings is especially important. Studies and testimony have shown that schools try to comply with legal mandates and procedures but have not made the effort to foster empowerment through collaboration (Green & Shinn, 1995; Turnbull & Turnbull, 1996; National Council on Disability, 1995). However, strategies for involvement are being pursued. They include increased efforts to involve families in the assessment process (Winton, 1994), and using collaborative conference techniques to increase parent and student participation.

Parent involvement can have a critical effect on the transition process from school to postschool activities. A study by Morningstar, Turnbull, and Turnbull (1995) found that families greatly influenced decisions made by students with disabilities. With regard to the transition process, students' perspectives about their vision for the future, how to plan for the future, and their self-determination were all influenced by their families. Most of the students based their career plans on input received from career planning courses in school. Although the IEP process requires transition planning (34 CFR 300.346(b)), with the current format used during IEP meetings, the majority of the students found the IEP process irrelevant. Morningstar et al., suggested that parent's and extended family members' viewpoints be incorporated into the IEP process in a more meaningful way.

SUMMARY

Parents have historically provided the force behind major changes in the field of special education. They formed local, state, and national organizations to promote the welfare of their children. They actively partitioned local, state, and federal agencies to legislate changes. Their efforts greatly assisted in passing federal legislation designed to improve the educational opportunities for all children with disabilities.

The most recent federal legislation (P.L. 105-17) has mandated the involvement of parents in the planning and implementation of individualized education program as well as to ensure that procedural safeguards for parents are fully explained. These legislation and court cases have had a significant impact upon regular and special education programs and related services.

Federal legislation also mandated that collaborative efforts be conducted between parents and professionals. Parents were no longer to sit passively and have professionals to dictate educational plans for their children. The law gave parents the right to be active participants in all assessment, placement, educational, and transition services. The legislation clearly indicated and validated involvement of parents and families in decisions about their child's education and is a central component of family-school collaboration.

REFERENCES

Bailey, D. B., Palsha, S. A., & Simeonnson, R. J. (1991). Professional skills, concerns, and perceived importance of work with families in early intervention. *Exceptional Children, 58*(2), 156-165.

Green, S. K., & Shinn, M. R. (1995). Parent attitudes about special education and reintegration: What is the role of student results. *Exceptional Children, 6*(13), 269-281.

Hardman, M. L., Drew, C. J., Egan, M. W., & Wolf, B. (1993). *Human exceptionality: Society, school, and family.* Needham Heights, MA: Allyn and Bacon.

Harry, B., Allen, T., & McLaughlin, M. (1995). Communication versus compliance: African American parents involvement in special education. *Exceptional Children, 61*(4) 364-377.

Mallory, B. L. (1996). The role of social policy in life cycle transitions. *Exceptional Children, 62*(3), 213-223.

McBride, S. L., Brotherson, M. J., Joanning, H., Whiddon, D., & Demmitt, A. (1993). Implementation of family-centered services: Perceptions of families and professionals. *Journal of Early Intervention, 17*(4), 414-430.

Morningstar, M. E., Turnbull, A. P., & Turnbull, H. R. (1995). What do students with disabilities tell us about the importance of involvement in the transition from school to adult life. *Exceptional Children, 62*(3), 249-260.

National Council on Disability. (1995). *Improving the implementation of the individuals with disabilities education act: Making school work for all American children.* Washington, DC: Author.

Shea, T. M., & Bauer, A. M. (1991). *Parents and teachers of children with exceptionalities: A handbook for collaboration.* Boston: Allyn and Bacon.

The National Center for Children and Youth with Disabilities. (1998). Number 26. Washington, DC: Author.

Turnbull, A. P., & Turnbull, H. R. (1996). *Families, professionals, and exceptionality*. Upper Saddle River, NJ: Merrill.

U. S. Department of Education. (1995). Individuals with disabilities education act amendments of 1995. Washington, DC: Author.

U. S. Department of Education. (1997). Individuals with disabilities education act amendments of 1995. Washington, DC: U.S. Government Printing Office.

Winton, P. J. (1994). Families of children with disabilities. In N. G. Haring, L. McCormick, & T. G. Haring (Eds.). *Exceptional children and youth* (6th ed.). New York: Merrill.

Chapter 6

TECHNIQUES FOR IMPROVING PARENTAL INVOLVEMENT

INTRODUCTION

Parental involvement is a widely accepted practice among proponents of education. Parents can serve as partners to the teacher in the child's academic program. Henderson (1998) summed up the importance of parental involvement in the schools by stating that parents are a school's best friend. She listed several statements which have major implications for involving parents in the school: (1) The immediate family, not the school, provides the first instruction for the child; (2) Parental involvement in their children's' education improves the child's chances for later academic success; (3) Parental involvement is most effective when it is comprehensively planned; (4) The earlier parents become involved in their children's education, the more likely they will be involved throughout the child's academic career.

It is incumbent upon the school to understand and appreciate the importance of parental and families' involvement in order to improve family/school cooperation. Individuals with disabilities cannot successfully reach their optimum level of functioning unless their parents become actively involved in their education (Taylor, 1998). Significant benefits can be derived from involving parents at any level.

It was commonly thought that parental involvement should be its strongest in the early school years, where strong foundations can be established. This view is expressed by many educators. Educators also support parental involvement and collaboration at the middle and secondary levels. Research tends to support that parental support is cumulative and the earlier parents are involved, the more successful the school experiences are (White & White, 1992; Finn, 1998; Epstein, 1995; Davies, 1996; Swick & Broadway, 1997).

To be effective, parental involvement must be launched on two fronts, the home and school. Involving parents with their children's education at home augments the learning process, providing that learning strategies are collaboratively addressed by both teachers and parents. Achievement of students tends to accelerate when both teachers and parents agree on common goals and objectives to be achieved. Parents can be instructed to focus on school readiness skills and specific objectives which nurture learning.

All children benefit when parents are involved in the school, this is especially true for children with disabilities and minority children. The education level of parents should not be a prerequisite for involving parents in the school. There are many nonacademic tasks that parents can perform. All children are pleased and proud to see their parents involved in the school (Wang et al., 1996; Floyd, 1998; Clark, 1993).

Both the home and the school have a significant impact on students' attitudes. Attitudes are mostly formed at home during the early years and are reinforced by the parents as the child matures. If attitudes are not reinforced by the school, negative ones may surface and impede the achievement of students.

DEVELOPMENT OF SCHOOL POLICY

Parental involvement in school policy is essential if the school is to meet state and federal mandates involving parents. We have devoted Chapter 10 to this topic. Parents should serve on all the major policy-making bodies in the school, not just the P.T.A. Parents should be involved in choosing textbooks, curriculum development, developing curriculum guidelines, social committees, and serving as resource individuals, to name but a few. Parental involvement appears most effective when parents are directly involved in all school activities that have a direct impact on their children. Parents can be effective when parents define the conditions under which they serve. Specific ways should be articulated how parents can participate in the education program. Some in-service training may be needed by parents to effectively participate in the education program (Thompson, 1998; Miller, 1998; Potter, 1996; Ohlrich, 1996).

Brandt (1998) wrote that schools cannot meet the challenges of reforms without first doing a better job of connecting with parents and the public. Strategies must be developed to reestablish public support for the public schools. The Education Commission of the States, in concert with new schools, conducted a parental survey to determine views toward education. Results supported that people wanted change but could not agree on what type and extent of change that was needed. In order to bring about effective changes and reforms in education, views and perceptions of parents must be an essential part of the formula.

Strategies recommended by the Commission of States (1996a) appear to be noteworthy of considering:

1. Listen to people first, talk later.
2. Expect to fail if you do not communicate well with teachers.
3. Make involving parents and the community a top priority.
4. Be clear about what it means to set high standards for all students, and what it will take to achieve them.
5. Show how new ideas enhance, rather than replace, the old ones.
6. Educate parents about the choices available to them.
7. Help parents and other community members understand how students are assessed and what the results mean.

Sergiovanni's views (1996) supported the Commission of the States position, in that he argued that both the what and how of student learning should be decided by teachers and parents, because that is the essence of democratic community and because the give-and-take of such discussions is what produces understanding and trust. Authenticity is essential in promoting trust between stakeholders. It is what parents desire most from the school (Rich, 1998). Educators assumed that parents expected them to be professional and businesslike; parents actually want the opposite. Parents from all levels complained about educators talking down to them (Commission of the States, 1996b).

Over the last several decades, the school has had a difficult time in establishing effective partnerships with parents. Much of the fragmentation has occurred because of noninvolvement, hostility, or parental indifference towards the school. Many schools serving parents of children with disabilities consider them a nuisance, unproductive, uneducated, lacking social graces, and not well-informed on education and social issues. The relationship is further strained when parents internalize negative behaviors displayed by the school. They frequently view the school as an unacceptable place, which has no interest in them as individuals. There must be a total shift in this paradigm. The school must accept these parents and provide training and assistance in desired areas, if the child's educational experiences are to be effective. Parents may also reinforce the academic and social skills taught at school by teaching them at home. They may also provide the school with valuable information concerning developmental issues, safety concerns, community resources, and demonstrations. Additionally, they may serve as resource individuals.

Effective parental involvement programs acknowledge the fact that parents are a child's earliest and most influential teachers. Attempting to educate the child without parental support is a kin to trying to rake leaves in a high wind.

COLLABORATIVE EFFORTS AT SCHOOL

The National Association for the Education of Young Children (NAEYC) has advocated programs to develop closer support between parents and teachers. Program goals should be developed in collaboration with families and the school staff. Parents should be equal partners in the formulating, implementing, and evaluating the effectiveness of programs for their children. It is commonly recognized today by the school that parental involvement is a necessary ingredient in the education of their children.

In order to improve parental involvement into early childhood programs, Powell (1998) stated that the process requires conceptual and structural provisions that enable all staff to maintain meaningful connections with families. The following provisions are recommended:

1. Early childhood programs serve families, not children alone. All policies should consider the impact they have on the family as well as incorporating information from the family and the direct involvement of family members.
2. Program practices in relating to parents must be in tune with widespread demographic changes, especially the characteristics and circumstances of families being served by the program. The cultural values, lifestyles, and customs of the families must be considered, respected, understood, and carefully integrated within the program.

3. Parent and teacher confidence in each other is the foundation of healthy relationships. Strategies must be implemented to assist in training parents and using the expertise of parents in the education programs. Using this approach, a twofold purpose is accomplished: (a) Parents are assured that practices are safe and conducted by competent teachers, and (b) Teachers are assured that parents strengths and competencies have been identified and used appropriately within the educational program.

4. Relations with parents should be individualized in a way that informs staff of the understandings of the work with each child. Ways of achieving the goals and objectives for children should be clearly articulated by teachers and parents. Parents and teachers should agree about content, resources, curricula, evaluation, and specific ways for achieving the stated goals and objectives of the program.

5. Programs should actively acknowledge parents as persons. The dignity of all persons should be respected, regardless of class, income, education, or racial or cultural values. The interests and needs of parents must be considered in any program.

6. Parents' beliefs may be as important as basic support for facilitating parent participation in meetings and other activities. Parents should be encouraged to participate in meetings. Their suggestions and recommendations should be considered in making decisions relevant to educating their children.

7. Definitions and assessment of the quality of an early-childhood program should give greater attention to parents' perspectives and to the program practices with parents and families. Parents have seldom been involved in defining and evaluating the scope of programs. They have valuable input to give and must be permitted to share their views. It is important that these views be reflected in programs.

8. Professional education and credentials should promote skills in relating to parents. Professional certification of teachers must be imposed. Part of the certification of teachers should be competencies required for effective work with parents, which is the major purpose of this text. Innovative strategies should be in place to increase parental involvement in the school.

Parental Involvement in the School

According to Kelley, Brown, Butler, Gittens, Taylor, and Zeller (1998), parental involvement in their school has been improved through looping. Looping was defined as a process for addressing the student's behavioral and social development. On the first day of school, the student, the parent, the teacher, and the administrator sign and begin to implement contracts for optimal learning. The agreement specifies the roles each participant will play in the performance of the child. The process has shown a decrease in suspensions, an increase in attendance, and a healthy bond among parents, teachers, and administrators.

Parents should feel welcome at schools and should be used to augment the school program by serving as volunteers. Performing a variety of tasks within the school, children are proud to see their parents involved in the schools. Roles of parents within the school should include more than cutting out posters, making bulletin boards, making photocopies, and participating in bake sales. Rather they should be included in virtually all aspects of the school program. School-wide involvement should include, but not be limited to, participating in evaluating programs, conducting surveys, serving as team leaders, selecting textbooks, developing courses, developing standards for dress codes, developing new report cards, and developing technology plans.

Many of the aforementioned tasks can easily be accomplished through what Cavarretta (1998) referred to as shared decision-making. Parents, teachers, community leaders, and administrators working in teams to resolve issues surrounding students' educational needs. The planning team is also empowered to assist in developing the schools' curriculum and other support services needs to achieve the goals and objectives of the curriculum.

Cavarretta (1998) summed up some problems associated with shared decision-making:

1. It can be hard to sell to entrenched staff members who have developed their own styles of operation.
2. Share decision-making may challenge individuals in their comfort zone, the so-called experts' viewpoints may be contested and challenged. (Refer to Chapter 8 for additional information on sharing.)

Parental involvement in the school can also be expedited through scheduling periodical conferences. This will provide opportunities for the teachers to assess the parents' skills and completeness for working in the classroom. As parents become familiar with the academic programs at school, they may reinforce the skills taught to their children at home. Under supervision, the parents may develop or establish an academic program at home to augment the school's program.

Armstrong (1991) informed us that parental involvement is essential in assisting the school in developing appropriate social and educational skills for individuals with disabilities. He concluded that involving parents in academic social skills homework makes transferring of skills functional and realistic for children with disabilities. The school should assure that parents are involved in:

1. The assessment process.
2. Instructional planning.
3. Decision-making.
4. Evaluation.
5. Identifying related service needs.
6. Selecting parenting skills.
7. Planning for support learning at home.
8. Strategies for parental education.
9. Ways for becoming better advocates for educational reforms.

Parental Involvement in the Classroom

As outlined earlier in the chapter, parents who conduct academic tasks in the classroom should receive some type of advanced preparation and orientation. During this orientation, parents should be provided with the school's mission, philosophy, and educational program. Additionally, they should be apprised of: (1) the class schedules, (2) the school calendar, (3) official meetings, (4) resources and supplies, (5) extracurricular activities, (6) in-service training and provisions for working parents, (7) conference schedules, (8) food and snacks, (9) evaluation and progress reports, and (10) advanced notices of services needed. Many parents can serve as valuable resources. Some have expertise and competencies in selected areas which can support the academic program (Graft & Henderson, 1997; Ohlrich, 1996; Miller, 1998; Thompson, 1998; Floyd, 1998).

Improving the Infrastructure Plan

Attempts have been made through this chapter to denote the importance of involving parents in the total school program. It is believed to achieve this goal, that the infrastructure of the school must be changed to educate and prepare parents for a variety of duties. Recommended activities and strategies should include:

1. A comprehensive understanding of the learning process by parents.
2. A committee consisting of some parents to assess parental needs in the school.
3. Development of syllabi to address the goals and objectives in the various school programs.
4. Recommending procedures for training and educating parents on their roles and functions in developing an infrastructure plan.
5. Development of an assessment plan to evaluate the effectiveness of training and the infrastructure plan.
6. Assigning duties and responsibilities for implementing strategies and the infrastructure plan, directly into the instructional plan in the classroom.

Parental Involvement in the Educational Process

The selection of content for any unit should be based on three broad considerations: (1) the significance of the content in attaining the purpose of the particular unit, (2) the importance of the content to society, and (3) the needs and interests of the learners (Henson, 1995). Curricula experiences, to be effective, must cover experiences under the three basic domains: cognitive, affective, and psychomotor. Parental resources should be sought and if parents have any experiences in the listed domains, they should be employed.

Parental Involvement in Improving Achievements of the Children

The importance of involving parents in developing and constructing curricula has been recognized for many years. Yet, their direct involvement has not been clearly evident in the school. A systematic plan is needed by teachers to assist parents in raising the achievement of their children. The following suggestions are recommended for teachers to employ to assist parents in assisting their children. Teachers should encourage parents to:

1. Set a definite time for study each day with not interruptions;
2. Provide the proper environment;
3. Provide the materials needed;
4. Require the student to organize school materials;
5. Require a daily list of homework assignments;
6. Provide support and guidance, if the child becomes discouraged or frustrated.

There is no universal agreement on the impact of parental involvement in school engagement on achievement of students. In-school engagement is defined as attending conferences, doing volunteer work, and attending school events, to name but a few. Some research has shown negative results, others have shown some positive results; (Finn, 1993; Ho & Williams, 1996; Taylor, 1996; Wolf, 1998; Whitefore, 1998).

A recent *Reader's Digest* poll revealed that strong families give children an edge in school. Children who socially participate with family functions scored higher on tests than those who did not. The survey also revealed that strong family ties improved self-image and confidence in children. The family is the cornerstone for success in later life. Parent education appears to play a role in how well the student performs in school.

The quality of family life appears to be significant factors in all of the groups. Children with disabilities from intact families performed better than those who lived only with their mothers. Strong family ties appear to reduce some of the anxiety faced by children with disabilities. Children with disabilities from families who attended church also scored higher on tests. In the opinion of the author, these conflicting research findings may be attributed to lack of empirical research design in conducting the research. It is firmly believed that carefully designed studies will show significant correlation between parental involvement and student achievement.

PARENTAL INTERVENTION AT HOME

In support of the author's views, parental involvement has been proven to be highly correlated with student achievement. Research findings have shown that differences in children's performance could be directly attributed to specific parental behaviors and interventions.

High achieving students usually had parents who constantly interacted with them, created conducive home environments, and provided emotional support to their children when they encountered failure, assisted children in managing and organizing their time, and were actively involved in homework, literacy, and reading at home (Wang, Haertel, & Walberg, 1993; Finn, 1993, 1998; Masten, 1994; Penn & Leo, 1992; Astone & McLanahan, 1998; Taylor, 1996, 1997, 1998; Ho & Williams, 1996; Edwards, 1992, 1995).

Additional research by the authors listed supports the view that children whose parents regularly converse with them on school-related matters perform better academically than children who parents do not discuss school issues. The relationship between parent and student is significantly improved when there is joint parent-student decision-making.

COMMUNITY INVOLVEMENT

Research has shown that community involvement and action can be powerful allies in transforming schools. Community involvement with the schools has been credited with: (1) improving the physical conditions and resources which support learning in the schools; (2) raising the attitudes and expectations of parents, teachers, and students; and (3) improving the depth and quality of the learning experiences of students through collaborative planning (Hatch, 1998; Shirley, 1997; Murnane & Levy, 1996; Vargas & Grose, 1998).

It is essential that parents be involved and informed about progress made toward achieving reforms. Parents are more likely to become associated with the school if educators develop a strong and trusting relationship with them. The bond can be further strengthened through making frequent contacts with the parents, conducting seminars, and sponsoring social events developed by the community.

It is important that the community assist parents as much as possible because of the emotional impact on the family. Services provided to parents by the community will impact to some degree how children with disabilities will develop, as well as providing strategies for family members to deal with the disabilities. The most important act a community can provide to families is a willingness to listen and understand what they are experiencing. It is essential for parents and siblings to have someone they can express their feelings to and receive support.

The need for direct involvement of parents and communities has been advocated by Atkinson and Juntunen (1994). They reported that school personnel must function as a school-home-community liaison. Casas and Furlong (1994) wrote that parental participation and empowerment in the community must be increased. Encourage parents to visit with other parents of children with disabilities. Most communities have support groups of parents who have disabled children. Organizations dealing with the specific disability of the child can also be helpful to the family (e.g., The Association of Retarded Citizens, United Cerebral Palsy Association). (See Appendix A for additional associations.)

Parents need to be reassured that they are competent individuals and parents. Encourage the parents to have a life of their own, to go out and to enjoy themselves. Offer to baby-sit so that the parents can have a period of relief. Encourage parents to use respite care facilities where children with disabilities can be cared for while they go out, go on a trip, or run an errand.

Parents should use a variety of community resources to promote social and academic experiences, through direct participation with their children with disabilities. Participating in community activities is one way for children to have fun while gaining practical experiences with peers (Taylor, 1998). Many communities offer a variety of activities designed to build social and academic skills such as:

1. Preschool story hour at the library;
2. Water play and swimming lessons;
3. Children's films;
4. Holiday parades;
5. Holiday parties;
6. Supervised play at "tot lots";
7. Dance classes;
8. Children's exhibits at museums;
9. Special events at shopping malls;
10. Community outreach centers;
11. Community fairs at neighborhood schools.

Not only do parents need community support, they also need reliable information from professionals involving their children with disabilities.

PARENTAL GUIDELINES FOR PROMOTING SOCIAL AND ACADEMIC GROWTH

Individuals with disabilities as well as all children follow developmental milestones in social skills. This sequence permits parents to work with their children where there are developmental problems and to pattern the learning of social and academic skills in a more predictable manner. It is commonly agreed that parents should be provided with as much information as possible concerning their children with disabilities. As indicated, Heddel (1998) recommended the following guidelines relevant to communicating diagnostic information to parents:

1. Parents should be told as soon as possible, preferably by a doctor. This information should be communicated in an appropriate place, such as an interview room or office.
2. There should be no casual observers—this is a private matter.
3. Both parents should be told at the same time. It should not be left to one parent to inform the other.
4. The newborn should also be in the room, if possible.
5. Parents should be given time and an opportunity to ask questions, even though they may be confused and at a loss for words.
6. Another interview should be scheduled, not more than a day or two later.
7. Parents should be encouraged to bring questions that will inevitably come up in the interim, and should be told that another person having experienced the specific type of disability will be at the next meeting to help answer questions and suggest some sources of help. Information is also needed on strategies that parents can employ in working with their children with disabilities at home.

SUMMARY

From the very beginning, children with disabilities should have an important place within the family structure. By being responsive to children's needs, parents build the foundation for interactive social relationships. The drive for independence emerges as developmental skills grow. As the child tries to do more and more for himself or herself, he or she continues to depend on the parents for guidance and support. Parents delight in the small accomplishments of a child can set expectations for larger success.

Parents of children with disabilities, as well as all parents, have a tremendous influence and impact on setting appropriate models for developing SOCIAL AND ACADEMIC SKILLS. The developmental sequence of tasks must be considered in social and academic training. Parents can contribute significantly to their children with disabilities' self-concept and control through appropriate modeling strategies as outlined in Chapter 2.

In order for parents of children with disabilities to be effective change agents in promoting appropriate social and academic skill development, early interventions in health care, counseling, housing, nutrition, education, and child-reading practices, etc. must be improved. Early intervention and parental involvement are essential for preparing children to master skills and tasks successfully.

There has been strong support from the federal government to include the family in the early educational process of their children. Parental involvement permits children to successfully manipulate their environments. The federal government created guidelines for the educational community in developing and implementing a comprehensive, coordinated, multidisciplinary, interagency program for early intervention services for infants, toddlers, and their families (Gallager, 1998).

The role of parental participation in the education of their children with disabilities, according to much of the research in the field, has shown limited participation between them and school. This view has been interpreted to imply by many that parents simply had no interest in the education of their children (Lyncy & Stein, 1987). Several factors may contribute to lack of parental participation and involvement. Many parents do not feel welcome in the schools. They believe that they have little to offer in the education of their children. Cassidy (1988) reported that problems with scheduling, transportation, and knowledge of instructional programs, (IEP) procedures are partly responsible for poor parental participation. Parents must be actively involved in all aspects of planning, including assessment, instructional planning, program evaluation, and monitoring programs. Special efforts are needed to develop better working relations from diverse parent groups.

The role of parents of children with disabilities in the schools must supersede the mandates of P.L. 94-142 and its amendments. Parents must feel that they are welcomed in the school and be given responsibilities concerning planning, collaboration with teachers, and involvement in policymaking. Parents should have an active role in the planning and instruction of their children and function as advocates for them if children are to profit significantly from their school experiences. Schools should experiment with various ways of improving parental participation, since parents are the foremost educators of their children.

REFERENCES

Armstrong, S. W., & McPherson, A. (1991). Homework as a critical component in social skills instruction. *Teaching Exceptional Children, 24*(1), 45-47

Astone, N. M., & Lanahan, S. S. (1998). Family structure, parental practices, and high school completion. *American Sociology Review, 56*(3), 309-320.

Atkinson, D. R., & Juntunen, C. L. (1994). School counselors and school psychologists as school-home-community liaisons in ethnically diverse schools. In P. Pederson & J.C. Carey (Eds.), *Multicultural counseling in schools: A practical handbook.* Boston: Allyn and Bacon.

Brandt, R. (1998). Listen first. *Educational Leadership, 55*(8), 25-30.

Casas, M., & Furlong, M. J. (1994). School counselors as advocates for increased Hispanic parents participation in schools. In P. Pederson & J. C. Carey (Eds.), *Multicultural counseling in schools: A practical handbook.* Boston: Allyn and Bacon.

Cassidy, E. (1988). Reaching and involving black parents of handicapped children in their child's education program (ED 302982). Eric Document Reproduction Service.

Cavarretta, J. (1998). Parents are a school's best friend. *Educational Leadership, 55*(8), 12-15.

Clark, R. M. (1993). *Family life and school achievement.* Chicago: University of Chicago Press.

Davies, D. (1996). Partnerships for student success. *New Schools, New Communities, 12*(3), 14-21.

Floyd, L. (1998). Joining hands: A parental involvement program. *Urban Education, 33*, 123-125.

Education Commission of the States. (1996a). *Listen, discuss, and act.* Denver, CO: Author.

Education Commission of the States. (1996b). *Bending without breaking.* Denver, CO: Author.

Edwards, P. A. (1992). Involving parents in building reading instruction for African-American children. *Theory Into Practice, 31*(4), 350-359.

Edwards, P. A. (1995). Combining parents' and teachers' thoughts about storybook reading at home and school. L.M. Morrow (Ed.) *In family literacy: Connections in schools and comunities.* College Park, MD: International Reading Association.

Epstein, J. L. (1995). School, family, community, partnerships: Caring for the children we share. *Phi Delta Kappan, 77*(9), 701-712.

Finn, J. D. (1998). Parental engagement that makes a difference. *Educational Leadership, 55*(8), 20-24.

Finn, J. D. (1993). *School engagement and students at risk.* Washington, DC: National Center for Educational Statistics.

Gallager, J. J. (1989). The impact of policies for handicapped children on future education policy. *Phi Delta Kappan,* 121-124.

Gough, P. B. (1991). *Tapping parent power.* Phi Delta Kappan, 72(95), 339.

Graft, O. L., & Henderson, B. (1997). 25 ways to increase parental participation. *High School Magazine, 4*, 36-41.

Hatch, T. (1998). How community action contributes to achievement? *Educational Leadership, 55*(8), 16-19.

Heddel, F. (1988). *Children with mental handicaps.* Ramsburg, Marlbourough, England: Crowood Press.

Henderson, A. T. (1988). Parents are a school's best friend. Bloomington, IN: *Phi Delta Kappa,* 135.

Ho, E. S., & Williams, J.D. (1996). Effects of parental involvement on eighth-grade achievement. *Sociology and Education, 69*(2), 126-141.

Kelly, P. A., Brown, S., Bulter, A., Gittens, P., Taylor, C., & Zeller, P. (1998). A place to hang our hats. *Educational Leadership, 56*(1), 62-64.

Lynch, E. W., & Stein, R. (1987). Parent participation by ethnicity: A comparison of Hispanic, Black, and Anglo families. *Exceptional Children, 54*, 105-111.

Masten, A. (1994). Resilience in individual development: Successful adaptation despite risk and adversity. In M.C.Wang & E.W. Gordon (Eds.) *Educational Resilence in Inner-City American.* Hillsdale, NJ: Erlbaum.

Miller, J. M. (1998). When parents meet: Teacher teams. *The Education Digest, 64*(4), 65-66.

Murnane, R., & Levy, F. (1996). *Teaching the new basic skills: Principles for educating children to thrive in a changing economy.* New York: The Free Press.

Ohlrich, K. B. (1996). Parent volunteers: An asset to your technology plan. *Learning and Leading with Technology, 24*, 51-52.

Penn, S. S., & Lee, R. M. (1992). *Home variables, parent-child activities, and academic achievement: A study of 1988 eighth graders.* Paper presented at the Annual Meeting of the American Education Research Association, San Francisco.

Potter, L. (1996). Making school parent-friendly. *Education Digest, 62*, 28-30.

Powell, D. R. (1998). Reweaving parents into early childhood education programs. *Education Digest, 64*(3), 22-25.

Rich, D. (1998). What parents want from teachers. *Educational Leadership, 55*(8), 37-39.

Sergiovanni, T. J. (1996). Leadership for the school house. San Francisco: Jossey Bass.

Shirley, D. (1997). *Laboratories of democracy: Community organizing for school perform.* Austin, TX: University of Texas Press.

Swick, K. L, & Broadway, F. (1997). Parental efficacy and successful parent involvement. *Journal of Instructional Psychology, 24*, 69-75.

Taylor, G. R. (1997). Curriculum strategies: Social skills intervention for young African-American males. Westport, CT: Praeger.

Taylor, G. R. (1998). *Curriculum strategies for teaching social skills to the disabled: Dealing with inappropriate behaviors.* Springfield, IL: Charles C Thomas.

Taylor, R. D. (1996). Adolescents' perceptions of kinship support and family management practices: Association with adolescent adjustment in African-American families. *Child Development, 32*(4), 687-695.

Thompson, S. (1998). Moving from publicity to engagement. *Educational Leadership, 55*(8), 54-57.

Vargas, B. C., & Grose, K. (1998). A partnership for literacy. *Educational Leadership, 55*(8), 45-48.

Wang, J., et al. (1996). The relationship between parental influence and student achievement in seventh grade mathematics. *School Science and Mathematics, 96,* 395-399.

Wang, M. C., Haertel, G. D., & Walberg, H. J. (1993). Toward a knowledge base for school learning. *Review of Educational Research, 63*(3), 249-294.

White, A. E., & White, L. L. (1992). A collaborative model for students with mild disabilities in middle schools. *Focus on Exceptional Children, 24*(9), 1-10.

Whiteford, T. (1998). Math for moms and dads. *Educational Leadership, 55*(8), 64-66.

Wolf, J. M. (1998). Just read. *Educational Leadership, 55*(8), 61-63.

Chapter 7

PROMOTING CULTURAL AWARENESS

INTRODUCTION

Strategies should be developed or in place to permit families with different cultural and linguistic backgrounds, having children with disabilities, to fully participate in the schools. Variables such a socioeconomic status, education level, and length of residence in the country should not promote stereotyping beliefs relevant to cultures (Wayman, Lynch, & Hanson, 1990). Hyun and Fowler (1995) provided examples on how cultural awareness can be enhanced by exploring one's own cultural heritage and examining the attitudes and behaviors that are associated with one's own culture. Teachers must become familiar with the child's culture and community (Powell, 1998).

If limited English is spoken, the school should have an interpreter present. An ideal person may be a leader in the cultural community, providing that the individual can speak and interpret both languages. In planning for meetings and conferences, the following steps are recommended by Hyun and Fowler (1995), Landon and Novak (1998):

1. Decide with the parent who will participate.
2. Encourage parents to bring people who are important to them.
3. Send a written notice of the meeting in the parents' native language.
4. Determine whether families need assistance with childcare or transportation.

Following the aforementioned steps will show respect for the parents and recognize their individual differences and cultural values. Parents need to feel that their cultural styles and language are valued knowledge and that this knowledge is needed and welcomed in the school. The school can assist those parents by providing training pro-

81

grams to assist them in understanding their roles in planning and understanding their rights as mandated under federal legislation. (See Appendix G for some strategies.) Any training program, to be successful, must incorporate the language and culture of the parents in order to prepare them to participate and contribute to the educational planning of their children (Gorman & Balter, 1997; Thorp, 1997).

Creative and innovative ways relevant to family involvement must be experimented with to improve parental involvement, especially for parents of children with disabilities (Mansbuch, 1993). Factors such as (1) diverse school experiences, (2) diverse economic and time constraints, and (3) diverse linguistic and cultural practices all combine to inhibit parental involvement. Diversity should be recognized as a strength rather than a weakness.

DIVERSE SCHOOL EXPERIENCES

For parents whose home language or culture differs substantially from the norm may be exposed to conflicting expectations about acceptable modes of behavior. This is particularly true for parents of children with disabilities. Some culturally-shaped learning is not within the acceptable ranges for most schools. Parents confronted with so-called "normal behaviors" frequently remark that their behaviors are not accepted by the schools. If the schools are to effectively serve the needs of parents from diverse cultures, radical reforms and strategies must be developed to address the following as advocated by Cross (1988):

1. An awareness and acceptance of ethnic difference;
2. Self-awareness of one's personal culture;
3. Recognition of the dynamics of differences;
4. Knowledge of the family culture;
5. Adaptation of skills.

In summing up Cross' (1988) provisions, it should be readily recognized that changes are needed in how educators define cultures. Strategies are also needed to address ways of adapting one's perception toward various cultures. Educators must develop sensitivity to parents who exhibit behaviors which are foreign to our culture and modify and adjust the academic to compensate for cultural differences. The school must change the basic Eurocentric Model in use out of respect for cultural diversity.

DIVERSE ECONOMIC AND TIME CONSTRAINTS

Many families of children with disabilities, due to the high cost of health care and maintenance, have limited funds due to several factors. One major factor is the one-family income. Due to the constant care and needs of a disabled child, only one parent can work and that is usually the father, if one is present within the home. Another factor deals with the type and nature of the employment. Many parents of children with disabilities hold low paying jobs, chiefly due to their lack of educational training. Money earned is used to maintain the family from day to day. These economical conditions in the family frequently take priority over concerns related to the child's education. Thus, activities related to school, such as homework, attending meetings, volunteering, or involvement in any school activities are not considered important by some parents. In essence, many parents feel that the times spent with academic matters are secondary to employment. Educators should consider the aforementioned and attempt to structure activities to include parents in the schools. The notion of employing some of these parents as lunch aides, crossing guards, paraprofessionals, consultants, and resource individuals should be considered.

DIVERSE LINGUISTIC AND CULTURAL PRACTICES

Parents are accustomed to certain ways of acquiring and transmitting information. These methods are usually different from those expected by the school or less adaptive in different cultural contexts. Parents may be relatively unprepared to learn new ways of expressing themselves in languages and cultural experiences different than their own. The schools should recognize and appreciate the cultural and linguistic styles of parents. Misunderstood cultural and linguistic practices can lead to misjudging the parents' language and culture style as inappropriate (Taylor, 1998).

The school should highlight the notion that each culture and language has made significant contributions to mankind. Establishing relationships and activities for parents from diverse cultural and language heritage should be encouraged and supported by the school. Multiculturalism and diversity should be accepted and respected (Atkinson & Juntunen, 1994; Casas & Furlong, 1994; Taylor, 1997, 1998).

The aforementioned research has clearly indicated the need for direct work with parents of children with disabilities. School personnel must act as a school-home-community liaison between all aspect of the multicultural environment.

PROMOTING CULTURE AWARENESS

According to Hyun and Fowler (1995), culture understanding and awareness may be expedited by the school, developing strategies for educators to self-examine their own attitudes and values associated with one's and other cultures to reinforce the concept that cultures are more alike then different; there are several commonalties among cultures. Specific strategies may be developed by the school to improve culture awareness of parents with children with disabilities. Some strategies may include interviewing parents and family members, examining their official records to verify experience and competencies, clarifying one's attitudes toward diverse cultures and resources relevant to various cultures, and developing association with various groups and members of diverse culture groups.

The school should stress that each culture style is different; however, there are similar characteristics which operate across all cultures. It is incumbent upon the school to recognize cultural styles and how styles determine one's behavior. School activities should reflect the richness and contribution each culture has made to improve the human condition.

Norton and Drew (1994) wrote that people of diverse cultural backgrounds have perspectives and beliefs regarding disabling conditions that may differ from those of the culture majority. The research also indicated that parents from some cultures have great difficulty accepting disabilities due to religious beliefs and values. The school must take these factors and more into consideration when planning educational activities for parents.

SUMMARY

Many parents, but especially parents of children with disabilities from minority groups, can find school an intimidating place (Lynch & Stein, 1987). Participation may be promoted by planning activities and inviting parents to school activities involving cultural experiences of their children. Cultural sensitivity, on the part of the school, is necessary if it is to effectively relate to the parents. Diversity should be recognized as strength rather than a weakness. Parents need to feel that their cultural styles and language are valued knowledge and that this knowledge is needed and welcomed in the school. The school can assist those parents by providing training programs to assist them in understanding their roles in planning for their children. Any training program, to be successful, must incorporate the language and culture of the parents in order to prepare them to participate and contribute to the educational planning of their children.

Collectively, some researchers attribute student success to parental involvement despite the adversities posed by poverty, minority status, or native language (Finn, 1993; Masten, 1994). In essence, some children succeed in spite of the environment or when parents are actively involved in the activities of the school. On the other hand, deprived environments can have significant impact on achievement of many children with disabilities. A case in point can be a home void of interesting books to read to students. These students may not have the skills to be successful in reading or completing school assignments (Edwards, 1995). The educational program of the school is strengthened when the cultural values of the parents are considered in educational planning.

REFERENCES

Atkins, D. R., & Juntunen., C. S. (1994). School counselors and school psychologists as school-home-community liaisons in ethnically diverse schools. In P. Pederson

& J.C. Carey (Eds.), *Multi-cultural counseling in schools: A practical handbook*. Boston: Allyn and Bacon.

Casas, M., & Furlong, M. J. (1994). School counselors as advocates for increased Hispanic parent participation in schools. In P. Pederson & J. Carey (Eds.), *Multi-cultural counseling in schools: A practical handbook*. Boston, MA: Allyn and Bacon.

Cross, T. (1988). Services to minority populations: What does it mean to be a culturally competent professional? *Focal Point, 2*(4), 1-3.

Edwards, P.A. (1995). Combining parents' and teachers' thoughts about storybook reading at home and school. In L.M. Morrow (Ed.), *Family literacy: Connections in schools and communities*, College Park, MD: International Reading Association.

Finn, J. D. (1993). *School engagement and students at risk*. Washington, D.C.: National Center for Education Statistics.

Gorman, J. C., & Balter, L. (1997). Culturally sensitive parent education: A critical review of quantitative research. *Review of Educational Research, 67*, 339-369.

Hyun, J. K., & Fowler, A. (1995). Respect cultural sensitivity and communication. *Teaching Exceptional Children, 28* (1), 25-28.

Langdon, H. W., & Novak, J. M. (1998). Home and school connections: A Hispanic perspective. *Educational Horizons, 1*, 15-17.

Lynch, E. W., & Stein, R. (1987). Parent participation by ethnicity: A comparison of Hispanic, Black, and Anglo families. *Exceptional Children, 54*, 105-111.

Mansbach, S. C. (1993). We must put family literacy on the national agenda. *Reading Today*, 37.

Masten, A. (1994). Resilience in individual development: Successful adaptation despite risk and adversity. In M.C. Wang & E.W. Gordon (Eds.), *Educational resilience in inner-city America*. Hillsdale, NJ: Erlbaum.

Norton, P., & Drew, C. J. (1994). Autism and potential family stressors. *American Journal of Family Therapy, 22*, 68-77.

Taylor, G. R. (1997). Curriculum strategies: Social skills interventions for young African American males. Westport, CT: Praeger.

Thorp, E. K. (1997). Increasing opportunities for partnership with culturally and linguistically diverse families. *Intervention in School and Clinic, 32*, 261-269.

Wayman, K. L., Lynch, E. W., & Hanson, M. J. (1990). Home-based early childhood services: Cultural sensitivity in a family systems approach. *Topics in Early Childhood Special Education, 10*, 56-75.

Chapter 8

SHARING INFORMATION

INTRODUCTION

Parents and teachers must share information so that systematic planning and instructional procedures are realistic. Sharing information will assist parents and teachers to assess the origin, degree, type, and location of the problem (James, 1996). The primary reason for sharing information is to determine if the problem is at school, home, community, or in several locations. Once the problem is identified, assistance can be made available. Another value of sharing information is for both parent and teacher to verify the information. Parents have a legal right to examine and contest any information relevant to their children. Chapter 5 addresses this issue in greater detail. Several sources may provide information for teachers and parents to share and validate: (1) cumulative records, (2) medical and social histories, (3) achievement test results, (4) mental abilities, and (5) physical growth and development.

These informational sources will provide a preponderance of information concerning children with disabilities and may be used:

- To share with parents their child's assessment information and describe his or her special and regular education programs.
- To ascertain parents' perceptions of their children and their exceptionality, as well as their special needs, prognosis, and educational programs.
- To determine parents' needs, desires, interests, and competencies in parenting their children and responding to their special needs.

Sharing information can lead to valuable insight on the part of both parent and teacher (Greer, 1996). A significant amount of information may be shared through a teacher-initiated conference.

TEACHER-INITIATED CONFERENCE

The teacher should have several general questions to pose to the parent during the interview, such as general demographics; physical characteristics; history of the disability; types of educational strategies and intervention to which the child has been exposed; personality traits; home and family behaviors; types of employment, if any; and other information not in the official school record, such as community services or out-of-state services.

Information can be collected and validated through the initial conference. Many learning and behavior problems can be addressed jointly by teachers and parents during this conference. Many problems can be posed and solved through collaboration. Teachers should be fully aware that regardless of the conditions in the home, the school cannot relinquish its responsibility in educating in the child. Situations which profit from collaboration may be classified into the following categories:

1. The student is not physically or emotionally available for learning. The physical or emotional problems are impeding learning, the parent or the teacher needs some direct intervention.
2. The student needs additional exposure to facilitate learning. Reinforced practice at home in the content areas, social skills, and physical skills are needed to reinforce skills taught at school. Some parental training may be in order.
3. The student's positive behavior should be reinforced. Strategies for reinforcing behavior should be a joint effort conducted by the school and home. Agreements should be made on the types of behaviors to enforce and the type and amount of reward to be given for certain behaviors.

Based on information from the initial interview, several types of conferences may be needed. This issue has been given special attention in Chapter 10. The following guidelines are designed to assist teachers in preparing for conferences and sharing information (Waler, 1998; Hamett, 1997).

1. Acquire knowledge from other professionals involving the past performance of the student.
2. Enlist information from school staff members to objectify information and observations.
3. Collaborate information with the family members, the education staff, community individuals, and specialists in the field to increase competence.

4. Acquire and share information with community agencies concerning the child, once parental permission has been obtained, or permission from a mentally able child over 18 years old.
5. Ethical procedures should be followed when sharing information within the school or agency. Parental permission is recommended when information from the classroom is shared with others within the school associated with the child's education.
6. Impress upon professionals, nurse, counselor, administrators, next year's teacher, the importance of the respect for confidentiality.
7. All recorded conference information should be available to parents upon request.
8. Any information which cannot be validated by parents should be discussed and removed, if so warranted.
9. Nonteaching staff and volunteers should be apprised of ethical standards for handling information.
10. Requests for information from outside agencies or individuals not remotely associated with the child's educational program must include written permission from the parent to release such information.
11. Personal and working notes are personal matters and should not be shared with others. The records should not be considered part of the child's official records. Some type of safeguard should be in place to protect the records. In rare instances, in the opinion of the teacher, personal notes may be shared if they will promote some aspects of the child's program.
12. Information which can be objectively verified or does not assist the student should not be included in reports.
13. At all cost, the teacher, as much as possible, should ensure that the protection and rights to privacy of those under his or her supervision are protected.

CONFIDENTIALITY

Information collected from sharing sessions and initial conferences related to children with disabilities must be treated in a professional and confidential manner. Information may not be distributed without parental permission. Parents should be assured that information revealed about their children will be treated as a private matter. Unless this is done, further cooperation and collaboration may be impeded. Every effort should be made to reassure parents that unless they agree to disclose specific information, what they tell is strictly confidential.

ROLE OF PROFESSIONALS

Professionals working with parents of children with disabilities should observe and respect confidential information, not only out of the respect for the parents, but because of laws which protect the rights of parents (refer to Chapter 5). Consequently, many aspects of confidentiality are being reviewed and reexamined by professionals. Some of the strategies employed by professionals to apprise parents of their rights include conducting workshops and symposia on the subject. Educators need to examine their strategies for assuring confidentiality of information and take a new look at the ethics which underpin their practices.

Strickland and Turnbull (1993) may provide standards for educators to employ. They articulated that public agencies must obtain parental consent before releasing personally identifiable information to anyone other than officials of the agency. Several safeguards were listed to protect the confidentiality of information:

1. Each public agency shall appoint one official with overall responsibility for ensuring confidentiality.
2. Training must be provided to all persons collecting or using personally identifiable information.
3. A list must be compiled and made available for public inspection by each agency containing the names and positions of all employees within the agency who may have access to personally identifiable information.

When the agency no longer needs the information, it must inform the parents that they have the option to request the destruction of the information. A permanent record, without regard to time constraints, involving demographic and academic information may be maintained.

IMPACT OF THE INFORMATION EXPLOSION

Technological advances and the information explosion age have made confidentiality of information an issue of concern for the relationships between individuals and institutions giving professional services and the client being served. Information electronically stored on children with disabilities can easily be retrieved by individuals other than professionals involved with the child or family. This has created serious problems in protecting privacy and human rights. Some of the changes responsible for a lack of security in confidential information may be attributed to the following factors:

1. Demands on accountability for the quality of services and third- party payment practices require extensive information and personal data about individuals served. Many people not involved in direct service to clients are employed in the data-gathering and evaluating process. Consequently, people know more about other people's affairs.
2. Modern technology not only has made vastly increased collections of data possible, but those data are now available and easily accessible.
3. Public concern is growing about the belief that professionals work in the best interest of individuals they serve. People are questioning how professionals use the information they gather about children with disabilities.
4. There is increased public awareness from parents that information constitutes power. Those who know about children with disabilities and their families have the power to use the information as they wish.
5. The "Rights" movement now including the Right to Privacy, expresses the nation's concern about information gathered and kept by institutions serving the disabled. Those records have the potential for far reaching impact on the lives of students with disabilities and their families. Parents can find out what information is kept and can challenge the accuracy of that information. Schools must make ethically and logically responsible decisions about data collection and storage to assure as much as possible the confidentiality of information entrusted in their care.

PRIVACY LAWS

In general, educators are in agreement with the aims of the various privacy laws. They recognize that abuses can occur in both public and private institutions. They are equally concerned with the fact that, in order to render quality service over a long period of time, schools must gather and share information with other professionals. It is illegal and unethical not to protect the privacy of parents by sharing information without parental approval. It is also unethical, though not illegal, to withhold information from other professionals who need that information to work effectively with parents of children with disabilities.

The Code of Ethics of the National Education Association adopted by the 1975 Representative Assembly states that " Educators...shall not disclose information about students obtained in the course of professional service...unless the disclosure serves a compelling professional purpose or is required by law" (Section 8, Principle 1).

Guidelines are needed by the National Education Association, similar to those posed by the American Psychological Association, to assist educators in protecting privacy of information gathered through conferences and collaborative efforts. Educators are mandated by law to secure information and to release information with parental approval. Assuring confidentiality of information does not direct teachers and professionals not to disclose information about students, but direct and require teachers and professionals with certain constraints to share information with professional individuals who need it to provide quality services to the parents of children with disabilities. Educators should be fully apprised that P.L. 94-142 guarantees confidentiality in the disclosure of information that may unnecessarily identify a student as having a disability.

SUMMARY

Most educators would agree that parents are the first teachers of their children. This view was supported by federal and state regulations, giving parents the ethical and legal right to be totally and completely involved in the education of their children. This includes sharing and validating information. Legal mandates for parental involvement have been articulated in chapter 5. At this point, an overview of the Buckley Amendment will summarize parental involvement relevant to releasing and challenging information in their children's reports.

The Buckley Amendment

The Buckley Amendment to Public Law 93-380 protects the rights and privacy of all students and parents. This legislation states that schools cannot release information or a child's record without parental consent. The amendment establishes parents' rights of access to their child's school records and the right to challenge information in the records they deem inaccurate or inappropriate.

Sharing information and initial conferences are essential to educational planning and conferences. Information gained through the sharing process can be used to developed collaborative agreements between parents and teachers. Specific techniques for using share information in collaboration are fully outlined in Chapter 10.

REFERENCES

Greer, M. H. (1996). The challenge of family involvement. *Exceptional Parent, 26,* 72.

Hamlett, H. E. (1997). Effective parent–professional communication. *Exceptional Parent, 27,* 51.

James, A. B. (1996). Helping the parents of a special needs child. *Lutheran Education, 32,* 78-87.

Strickland, B., & Turnbull, A. P. (1993). *Developing and implementing program* (3rd ed.). Englewood Cliffs, NJ: Prentice-Hall.

Swideret, B. (1997). Parent conferences. *Journal of Adolescent and Adult Literacy, 40,* 580-581.

Waler, J. A. (1998). Promoting parent/community involvement in school. *Education Digest, 63* (8), 45-47.

Chapter 9

REPORTING PROGRESS TO PARENTS

INTRODUCTION

Reporting progress of children with disabilities to parents requires some modification in the regular grading procedures. Modifications should be based upon the unique disability and interest of the child if needed. Many children with disabilities will not need any modifications in the grading procedures used. Any modifications made should resemble the regular grading system as much as possible. Strickland and Turnbull (1993) concluded that maintaining similar grading procedures for all students can serve to protect the student's right to confidentiality.

It is incumbent upon the teacher of children with disabilities to develop effective reporting procedures for informing parents of the progress of their children with disabilities. Reports to parents can also improve communication between the home and school. There are several reporting techniques that teachers may employ to inform parents. These techniques are chosen based upon the disabilities, needs, and interests of the children with disabilities; they are by no means inclusive.

1. ***Anecdotal Records.*** Anecdotal records may be used to show progress of students. A permanent type of folder should be used, such as a spiral notebook, to keep information. All relevant information concerning the student can be listed and categorized. Information listed in anecdotal records may provide information needed to justify a change in the student's academic program. Teachers should attempt to control being subjective in their interpretation of behaviors.

2. ***Work Samples.*** Work samples are excellent to use in comparing a student's performance between time periods on any area or areas in his or her academic program. Students can plot their own progress by

using work samples. Parents can also have an objective method to gauge their children's progress in school.

3. *Checklist.* The teacher records critical behaviors he or she has observed in the educational setting. Information is forwarded home to the parents. The parents' signatures denote that they have read the information included in the checklist. Collective strategies can be developed by the teacher and parents to reduce or eliminate the undesirable behavior or, in some instances, to promote possible behavior.

4. *Newsletters.* A newsletter is an excellent communication device for apprising parents about school issues and special events to be conducted at the school. The newsletter is an excellent device for seeking cooperation from parents in conducting certain school functions.

5. *Daily or Weekly Report Cards.* These report cards inform parents about the academic progress of their children. Parents have an opportunity to respond to the report cards and to indicate ways in which they can assist the child or to make other relevant comments.

6. *Telephone Calls.* Most telephone calls to parents are negative; frequently the teacher should have positive remarks to make.

7. *An Award System.* This system awards children for their accomplishments. The nature of the disability and the interest and needs of the children are considered. No group standards are employed. The child becomes his or her own yardstick and is awarded based upon achieving his or her individualized behavior.

8. *Use of Cameras and Videotapes.* The behaviors of students are recorded. The recordings and pictures may be used with the permission of parents. The recordings and pictures may be used by the teacher and parent to reinforce positive behaviors or to remediate negative behaviors.

9. *Use of Computer Technology.* This technology affords rapid reporting to parents, providing the parents have the necessary computer hardware and software and are versed in their uses.

10. *Home Visits.* Conditions in some communities do not make home visits an attractive option to many teachers. Some teachers, in spite of poor community conditions, visit homes. It is recommended, if home visits are conducted, that homes be visited before dark and that another individual accompany the teacher.

One of the first strategies advocated by Shea and Bauer (1991) is that teachers should contact the family as soon as possible, using some of the listed techniques outlined earlier. The benefits of this contact can be immeasurable in that parents can: (1) inform the teacher about changes in the developmental sequence of the child which may have an impact upon school performance; (2) assist the teacher in understanding the student's performance outside of the school that may have an impact upon performing in school; (3) shed light on culture differences which may be impeding the instructional program; and (4) assist in reinforcing skills learned at school, monitoring homework. Reporting data recorded and forwarded to parents should provide for parental disagreement. Any disagreements can be addressed at conference time (James, 1996; Voor, 1997).

REPORTING TO PARENTS

Parents have the right of securing information relevant to the function of their children in school. The legal aspects of parents' rights have been addressed in Chapter 5. The teacher's major responsibility is informing parents how well their children have progressed within a reporting period. Reporting periods should describe children's progress accurately and objectively. Teachers need to describe in narrative terms and provide samples of classwork so that the parents can make their own assessment of their children's work (Potter, 1998; Green, 1998).

Teachers, as indicated, have several avenues for reporting children's progress to parents. Before forwarding a report home or conducting a conference, educators should prepare an outline and include information which will reflect significant aspects of the child's behavior. Communication should be clear and concise. Language usage must be on a level which the parent can understand; if the language is not native English, attempts should be made to report to the parent in his or her native language. If this is not feasible, an interpreter should be available, so that parents may effectively participate and interact with the educator. Progress reports for children with disabilities are usually long narrative descriptions of behavior, constituting significant pages. To summarize the total report will consume too much time. The educator should select parts of the report which he or she wishes to discuss or forward home to the parents.

Frequently in conferences, educators and teachers have special concerns. These concerns may be completely independent of the information covered in the report. To avoid this type of encounter, educators should seek from parents their special interests. Another approach would be to have a planning meeting and to set the agenda at that time, or the educator can seek permission to explore an issue which in his or her opinion is common to the parents (Goldring & Hausman, 1997). Chapter 10 describes the various types of conferences and the importance of collaboration. Parents should keep in close contact with the school, regularly check their children's homework, and frequently send notes to school inquiring about the progress of their children. Parents displaying these traits are usually familiar with the school's program. These parents do not need a full conference or reporting period. Educators can simply review the major parts of the report and enlist comments from the parents. On the other hand, parents who do not frequently visit the school or keep in contact with it will need additional time and information concerning the school's program and reporting system.

Most parents like a reporting system which covers all of the aspects of human behavior, in the academic, social, emotional, and physical domains. Additionally, they are seeking information relevant to classroom behavior, normative data on performance, progress report on growth in all areas, and preferred learning styles. As outlined, some parents will need detailed information concerning the above. Others who are well informed will need little information. Educators will have to decide upon the best structure for reporting the information to the parents. Chapters 6 and 10 provide some insights.

ACADEMIC PERFORMANCE

The school should decide upon the frequencies of the reporting period; it may be weekly, monthly, quarterly, or every semester. Regardless of the reporting period, parents of children with disabilities, as well as all parents, are concerned about their children's academic performance in the basic skills as well as in other subjects. Teachers should provide objective information to parents in the academic areas through conferences and the reporting period. Parents should respond to the progress report. Collectively, parents and teachers can plan to develop strategies for improving the performance, or plan to upgrade or remediate the deficit areas. Planning may take place using a variety of approaches already articulated. It is the opinion of this author that a face-to-face conference is the better approach to take. The conference approach permits both teachers and parents to openly discuss their feelings and to collective by plan to address the problems of the child.

SOCIAL/EMOTIONAL DEVELOPMENT

Social/emotional competency is an important aspect of interrelationships (Taylor, 1998). The experience of interacting with others is necessary for the existence of all children, especially for children with disabilities. These children need to be acknowledged, noticed, valued, respected, and appreciated by others and to be aware that others want the same from them. Social/emotional competency is the sum total of one's ability to interact with other people, to take appropriate social initiatives, to understand people's reactions to them, and to respond accordingly (Taylor, 1998; Woeppel, 1990; Bryan, 1991). Children with disabilities must learn to appropriately interact with others. Social/emotional skills are a continuous process; parents need to know how their children's competency measures up and how they deal with their frustrations and approach new learning tasks. The teacher's progress report can indicate needed interpersonal skills to encourage and those to limit. Parental responses and practicing social skills at home can do much to augment the teacher's social skills program.

PHYSICAL DEVELOPMENT

Many children with disabilities have severe physical problems due to deficits in bones, nerves, muscles, and other organs. Many activities are restricted due to physical disabilities. Teachers should provide to parents detailed descriptions of physical activities the child can perform and provide as many physical activities as possible to assist in maintaining and developing whatever physical strength the child has. During reporting times, the teacher should discuss with the parents the strengths and weaknesses observed and a unified plan for meeting the stated goals for the child (Taylor, 1999).

Once the academic, social/emotional, and physical traits have been appropriately assessed, the next step for teachers and parents is to decide what strategies are to be implemented to achieve the stated objectives in each of the three major areas. The classroom is an excellent place for the child to demonstrate behaviors in the three domains outlined (Taylor, 1999).

CLASSROOM BEHAVIOR

The classroom provides a structure for the child to demonstrate various behaviors in the three basic domains (Taylor, 1999). Teachers need to make known to parents, methods and procedures, which will be employed to evaluate the child's behavior and performance. This assessment requires professional judgment on the part of the teacher to accurately and objectively report the behavior. Detailed knowledge of development norms in the areas of intelligence, social/emotional and physical development are needed in order for the teacher to make a valid report on the child's classroom behaviors. Parents should have an opportunity to observe the child in the classroom. They should plan with the teacher strategies for improving or modifying the behavior. When communicating with parents relevant to classroom behaviors, the teacher can compare performance of the child with another child of the same age. However, some caution is in order. Children of the same age with disabilities and having the same disabling conditions may perform well above or below the normative group. The recommended approach would be to use the child as his or her own yardstick and assess his or her learning styles to progress over a certain time frame.

During reporting and conference time, the teacher should discuss with the parent the procedures used to evaluate the child, noting reasons why the child is performing above or below the expected age level of his or her peers and how the learning style was assessed. It is essential, during the conference, that the teacher accent the positive behaviors of the child and encourage the parents to reinforce those behaviors at home. For negative behaviors, strategies should be discussed to minimize or eradicate the behaviors. Before ending the discussion, reporting period, or conference, teachers and parents should agree on the following:

1. What can be done at school and home to increase the child's performance in all academic, social/emotional, and physical development?
2. Timelines and location for the next conference with a possible area for discussion.
3. What community resources can be used to assist in meeting the stated objectives?
4. A plan for selecting a group leader, not necessarily the teacher.
5. Who will report to parents and to those who were not present at the initial conference?
6. Parents should leave the meeting with a tentative progress report on how certain strategies will be achieved.

SUMMARY

The teachers become the central figures in grading and reporting procedures employed in their schools. They are exposed to pressures from parents, children, and the school's grading policy for children with disabilities. The teacher becomes a catalyst in the grading and reporting controversy, attempting to explain the school's reporting pattern, and the unfeasibility of grading children with disabilities. Research is desperately needed to shed light on this matter. However, the school should make sure that parents understand the grading and reporting procedures employed and attempt to seek community support concerning their system.

Reports children with disabilities receive deviates from school district to school district, as well as from state to state. The use of reporting and grades in evaluating the progress of children with disabilities is highly questionable. Much of the controversy lies in the fact that administrators in the past had no objective or scientific system to determine the achievement of children with disabilities. The lack of specificity and objectivity of outcomes to be graded and the attitudes of teachers toward pupil interest and effort reduces decidedly the validity and reliability of marks. The value of a marking system subsequently becomes dependent upon what is being marked, who is doing the marking, who is being marked, and who interprets the marks. Furthermore, marks and accompanying competitive situations can cause many undesirable traits and attitudes to develop in children with disabilities, such as insecurity, fear, anxiety, cheating, and inferiority. These factors indicate that an objective and scientific way of evaluating the growth of these children should be instituted. Rather than group evaluation, individual evaluation based upon the unique interests abilities, disabilities, and characteristics of children with disabilities will aid in their total development. It is recommended that the approach outlined will better provide administrators and teachers with a model that will lead to effective evaluation of the children's achievement.

There is universal agreement that parents should be regularly informed by the school concerning their children's growth and development. The major source of conflict is how should this progress be reported. Administrators should endeavor to explain their grading systems to parents and to seek their support and approval before instituting any grading pattern. Teacher/parent conferences appear to be an opportune place to explain and seek parental approval for a marking system.

There are many ways of reporting to parents. Some of these ways include report cards, use of descriptive words, checklists, narrative or letter reports, conferences, pupil self-appraisals, informal notes, telephone conversations, information meetings, and home visits. It is maintained that as long as parents and school administrators agree upon a marking pattern, and parents understand that their children's achievement is evaluated in relation to their capacities, much of the controversy over marking will be significantly reduced. Reporting can then be viewed as a suitable method of helping parents to accept their children for who they are, and to understand what the school program is attempting to accomplish, and to learn how well their children are succeeding. Reporting should be a means for strengthening a sound relationship between home and school in the guidance of the child and contribute to the increased effectiveness of learning.

REFERENCES

Goldring, E. B., & Hausman, C. (1997). Empower parents for productive partnership. *Education Digest, 62,* 25-29.

Green, R. (1998). A parent's perspective. *Exceptional Parent, 28*(8), 32-33.

James, A. B. (1996). Helping the parents of a special needs child. *Lutheran Education, 132,* 78-87.

Potter, L. (1998). Making parent involvement meaningful. *Schools in the Middle, 6,* 9-10.

Shea, T. M., & Bauer, A. M. (1991). *Parents and teachers of children with exceptionalities: A handbook for collaboration* (2nd ed.). Boston: Allyn and Bacon.

Strickland, B. B., & Turnbull, A. D. (1993). *Developing and implementing individualized education programs*. Englewood Cliffs, NJ: Prentice-Hall.

Taylor, G. R. (1998). *Curriculum strategies for teaching social skills to the disabled*. Springfield, IL: Charles C Thomas.

Taylor, G. R. (1999). *Curriculum models and strategies for educating disabled children in inclusive settings*. Springfield, IL: Charles C Thomas.

Voor, R. (1997). Connecting kinds and parents to school. *Education Digest, 62,* 20-21.

Woeppel, P. (1990). Facilitating social skills development in learning disabled and / or attention deficit disorder second to fifth grade children and parents. Ed. D. Practicum. NOVA University.

Chapter 10

STRATEGIES FOR IMPROVING COLLABORATION BETWEEN PARENTS AND THE SCHOOLS

INTRODUCTION

Historically, parents have not been actively involved in the schools. Several reasons may be attributed to the position taken by some parents. Over the last several decades, the school has had a difficult time establishing effective partnerships with parents. Much of the fragmentation has occurred because of noninvolvement, hostility, or parental indifference toward the school. Many schools serving parents of children with disabilities consider them a nuisance, unproductive, uneducated, lacking social grace, and not well informed on educational issues. Today, due largely to federal and state legislation and local and national parental groups serving children with disabilities, the schools have been forced to involve parents in all aspects of their programs (Taylor, 1999).

Parents, as well as teachers, feel the impact of disparities between home and classroom environments (Griffith, 1998). They encounter tensions between what schools expect and do and their own practices at home, both indirectly through messages that their children bring home and directly through their own interactions with teachers and other school personnel. Materials that children bring home, often in the form of homework, inform parents about their children's capabilities and engage them in forms of interaction that they would have been unlikely to initiate on their own (Powell & Diamond, 1995; Penn, 1992; Wang, 1993; Gough, 1991; Clark, 1993). Parents' perspectives on home-school incompatibility have received even less attention than those of teachers. Available evidence is largely anecdotal and typically collected in conjunction with parent-focused intervention efforts.

Parents were also discussed as critical informants in teachers' efforts to interpret their students' classroom behaviors. Efforts aimed at reducing linguistic and cultural impediments to parents' involvement in their children's early education settings were widely applauded. Those familiar with such efforts reported that parents typically respond very positively to efforts to include them. When attempts at inclusion are not considered relevant to education, awkward encounters between parents and schools can occur (Masten, 1994; Casas & Furlong, 1994; Cassidy, 1988).

Issues associated with language differences between home and school are a particularly controversial topic of inquiry that, again, has largely ignored the parents' point of view (Lunch & Stein, 1987; Cummings, 1994). Research on bilingual education, for example, has focused on children's language outcomes to the neglect of effects on children's relations with their parents. Workshop participants raised concerns about the possible threat posed to non-English-speaking parents when their child's school entry coincides with immersion in English. These parents may experience two levels of loss, one associated with the children's departure from home and the other associated with fears that their ability to communicate with their children will be compromised. It is commonly recognized that most parents will need some type of plan in order to assist their children with disabilities standards advocated by the National PTA Organization.

THE PTA'S NATIONAL STANDARDS

The National PTA Organization has developed new guidelines that support the need for family involvement in the schools, premised upon the belief that parents are a child's first teacher. There is a body of knowledge which supports the notion that increased parental and family involvement leads to greater student performance. This concept is supported by the National PTA Association. In 1997, the Association developed the National Standards for Parental/Family Involvement Program to assist schools, communities, and parental groups to implement affective parent involvement programs with the goal of improving students' academic performance (Epstein, 1995).

The standards included (1) regular communication between home and school, (2) support in parenting skills, (3) an emphasis on assisting student learning, (4) the promotion of volunteering at school, (5) parent involvement in school decision making and advocacy, and (6) collaborations with the community to provide needed resources. These standards provided the indicators used by the National PTA to recommend the following procedures for improving parent and family involvement in the school:

1. Create an action team involving all stakeholders in reaching a common understanding and setting mutual goals.
2. Examine current practices; survey stakeholders' perception on current practices; modify, adapt, or make recommended changes.
3. Develop a plan of improvement based upon the data generated in #2.
4. Develop a written parent/family involvement policy based upon the goals and mission statement.
5. Secure support and financial resources needed to achieve the goals and to support the mission statement.
6. Provide professional development for school/program staff. Effective updated training is essential so that stakeholders may be abreast with the latest trends and innovations.
7. Evaluate and revise the plan. The plan should be a fluid document and changes made based upon evaluative results.

According to Sullivan (1998), using the National (Standards) as a model will permit schools, parents, and other stakeholders to develop and implement strategies to improve students' performance and encourage students to have more positive and healthier attitudes toward learning and school. Several other suggestions have been advanced by researchers in the field relevant to parental participation and collaboration (Giannetti & Sagarese, 1997-98; Kines, 1999; Wilson, 1997; Graves, 1996; Shea & Bauer, 1991; Perk, 1995; Ainsworth, 1996; Mills & Bulach, 1996; Marsh, 1999; Lewis & Morris, 1998; Floyd, 1998; Hatch, 1998; Whiteford, 1998; Wolf, 1998).

TACTICS FOR IMPROVING COLLABORATIVE EFFORTS

Some recommended tactics for improving parental involvement and collaboration have been advanced by Giannetti and Sagarese (1997-1998). They include:

1. Developing strategies for making parents more welcome in the school by inviting them to share their expertise with the classroom, hosting ethnic lunches, serving as chaperones, and tutoring children in academic subjects.
2. Advertising your expertise by letting parents know that you are competent in your designated areas.
3. Implementing an early warning system to inform parents of possible problems that children may encounter and provide strategies for correcting problems or performance before the children fail.
4. Accenting positive behaviors of the child rather than negative behaviors when reporting or conferring with parents.
5. Finding a common group to converse with parents by using their ethnic, religious, and cultural values.
6. Providing a safe environment by reassuring parents that their children will be safe in the classroom. Show parents some strategies that may be employed to protect their children.
7. Sharing with parents information that their children demonstrate in the classroom. Compare behaviors shown at home with school, such as information in anecdotal records.
8. Showing empathy, not sympathy, to parents. Empathy can assist the parents in dealing realistically with the problem, whereas sympathy appears to compound the negative aspect of the problem.
9. Being an effective and fair disciplinarian by applying the consequence of behavior equally to all who disregard the established rules.
10. Being a consistent role model that children can imitate and model. The National PTA Standards and the aforementioned tactics can be effectively used in planning a supportive collaborative program. These tactics can easily be employed with parents of children with disabilities with little or few modifications.

COLLABORATIVE PROBLEM-SOLVING TECHNIQUES

Collaborating with parents is a continuous process. There are several structures where effective collaborative strategies may be conducted, such as problem-solving groups and discussion groups. Most problems can be effectively addressed in conference settings (Kines, 1999; Wilson, 1997; McLaughlin, 1987; Graves; 1996; Steward, 1996).

Problem-Solving Groups

Parents who have similar problems related to their children may form groups to address them. These groups should be designed to discuss and recommended strategies for solving problems of their children with disabilities. The teacher should assess his or her abilities to lead such a group. If in the opinion of the teacher, he or she does not have the necessary skills or training to conduct the sessions, he or she should get a competent individual, skilled in counseling, such as a counselor, social worker, or school psychologist. The teacher should remain in the group and participate and assist in facilitating the process.

A planned systematic approach is needed for the facilitator to conduct the meeting. A first approach is to define the problem and receive universal acceptance of its definition and identification of individuals associated with the problem (refer to Appendix H for a survey form to identify problem areas). The second approach should be designed to develop a plan for solving the problem. Group members should discuss possible solutions, identify individuals needed, time, incident, and location relevant to the problem. Key individuals, including the teacher and parent, should be requested to provide strategies to address the problem; group consensus should be required. A third approach is to implement the plan as outlined. 1Specific strategies are jointly developed to assist the child with a disability. Some possible strategies may be:

1. That the teacher allow additional time on task;
2. That the child be placed in a different group or structure;
3. That additional related services be provided;
4. That a special instructional procedure be implemented;
5. That support is given for homework;
6. That a quiet place be provided for the child to study;
7. That social skills development be enforced at home;
8. That appropriate community resources be identified and used.

The nature and source of the problem will determined with specific strategies to implement. The above are merely suggestions which may or may not apply to individual children.

Discussion Groups

Discussion groups may follow the same format employed in problem-solving groups. The nature and purposes of the groups are uniquely different. As indicated in problem-solving groups, there are some group issues and problems to be jointly solved. This discussion group is based upon problems or information which have been initially agreed upon by the group. The group assembles to discuss and reach consensus about solving a problem. Each opinion is valued and considered. The teacher may initially serve as the group leader. As structure is developed, another group leader may be selected and the teacher's role may change to a resource person. For additional information concerning the purpose, objective, and structure of discussion groups, the reader is recommended to consult Shea and Bauer (1991).

Preparation for the Problem-Solving Conference

Before a problem solving conference is conducted, there is certain groundwork or preparation needed to be made by the teacher and parent. This approach improves the collaborative efforts and greatly assists in reducing or remediating the problem presented by the child. Before the problem-solving conference:

1. Identify the student's behavior which needs modification.
2. Determine what strategies the teacher will use at school.
3. Determine what the parent will do at home to reinforce the teacher's program.
4. Determine the effects of the teacher's behavior on the problems.
5. Determine the effects of the parent's behavior on the problems.
6. Identify alternative strategies for solving the problems.
7. Agree upon rewards and reinforcement to use in modifying behaviors.
8. Develop jointly an action plan, identifying step, timing, and human and physical resources to be implemented at school and home.

Develop follow-up strategies and an evaluation plan to evaluate the results of the conference (Perl, 1995; Ainsworth, 1996).

The Problem-Solving Conference

The problem-solving conference is a technique that teachers and parents can use collaboratively to solve behavior problems of children with disabilities once rapport has been established. In the opinion of the teacher, the parent may not have the necessary skills or knowledge to actively participate. In such a case, it is strongly recommended that the teacher train the parent so that effective collaboration can begin (Mills & Bulach, 1996; Gruan, 1990; Woeppel, 1990).

Problem-solving conferences should clearly indicate to teachers and parents that the child many not have problems in all segments of his or her collegial environment. A major aspect of problem solving is to determine which environment the behavior is occurring, such as school, home, in the community, or in several places. Once the environment associated with the behavior has been identified, systematic and collaborative planning can take place.

Guidelines for Conducting Problem-Solving Conferences

1. Describe the behavior in objectives and measurable terms.
2. Outline strategies to be used to reinforce behaviors.
3. Promote the use of all available information, including information from the home relevant to the problem.
4. Agree that all participants have equal rights.
5. Indicate how the parents may assist in the program.
6. Approval of the plan requires that all participants endorse it.
7. A commonly agreed reporting and grading policy should be intact.
8. Indicate specific ways for evaluating the plan based upon the results. Some indication of the next steps to be used should be outlined.

ROLE OF THE COMMUNITY

It would be neglectful not to explore the role and dimensions of the community in problem solving. A desirable relationship between school, home, and community is one that is marked by a strong bond of understanding and cooperation between parents and school personnel. Parents should have a direct share in deciding what problem-solving techniques appear to service their children best. Parents should be welcome to make suggestions for the guidance of their children. Through various channels, the school can improve collaboration for children with disabilities through the cooperation of parents and the community.

It has been commonly stated that no effective program can operate successfully for children with disabilities unless there is common understanding between various segments of the community and parents. All necessary information concerning the education of the child should be collaborated with the parent. Parents and the community should have direct input into the development of a program. For teachers and related school personnel, collaboration should involve the utilization of information from parents and community to develop instructional programs (Lewis & Morris, 1998; Floyd, 1998; Hatch, 1998).

Booth and Dunne (1996); Cairney, Ruge, Buchanan, Lowe, and Munsie (1995); and Epstein (1991) all concurred that effective collaboration implies more than simply establishing links with the home; rather, it requires a comprehensive and permanent program of partnership with families and communities. March (1999) summarized some of the values of partnership or collaboration between the home, the community, and the school. Effective partnerships or collaboration can improve:

1. School climate and programs;
2. Family support services;
3. Parents skills and leadership;
4. Family and community relationships;
5. Teacher effectiveness.

COLLABORATIVE PLANNING

Research by Thomas (1998) clearly indicated that gaining public and professional support for the school involves developing strategies that incorporate widespread participation in the development of standards by stakeholders. Some of the strategies could be designed to assist teachers in drafting district-wide standards (Education Commission on the States, 1996a).

Parental leadership skill workshops should be instituted to enable parents to become active participants in developing standards and educational decisions. Stakeholders who develop standards must share mutual commitments and responsibilities. Before enacting standards, the wider community should be informed and given its endorsement. The school must show concern and respect for all participants regardless of class, education, or diversity (Davies, 1996). This approach assures that democratic views and values are considered in educational planning.

Collaborative planning should be more than mere discussions and suggestions given by stakeholders. Rather, they should be engaged in developing strategies to bring about educational reforms and changes. Research findings tend to support that home to school collaboration is essential to the academic success of students. Collaborative arrangements increase parental decision-making and provide opportunities for school personnel to support parents in assisting their children to learn. Parents who have a conceptual understanding of the subject matter taught can better assist the child and augment the teacher's teaching strategies (Whiteford, 1998; Wolf, 1998).

A unique way for improving parent/teacher collaboration is to develop teams consisting of both parents and teachers. Miller (1998) offered the following suggestions for improving parents/teacher teams:

1. Be in touch long before the conference;
2. Be direct and personal in arranging the conference;
3. Be accommodating and try not to take no for an answer. Be flexible in setting meeting times around parents schedules;
4. Be on time;
5. Be prepared with handouts and work samples;
6. Be specific about problems;
7. Be knowledgeable as a team about each student;
8. Be welcoming;
9. Be in charge;
10. Be supportive;
11. Consider student-led conferences, which can be very effective for positive home-school relations;
12. Follow-up. Hold a team meeting to develop strategies for following up recommendations from the team; assign duties and responsibilities.

Team interaction is important and essential for improving the education of children with disabilities. This interaction can better assist the team in understanding the strengths and weaknesses of the child under study. The team may also act as an advocate for the child and assure that significant support is available to enable the disabled child to achieve his or her stated objectives.

PLANNING A SUPPORT PROGRAM

Collaboration involves planning, training, and identifying one's roles and responsibilities in achieving commonly developed goals and objectives. Several steps are advocated in order for collaborative activities to be successful. A first step should be to develop a detailed collaborative plan with timelines and general guidelines for the school year. The collaborative agreement will require a great deal of brainstorming and commitment of time and resources. A second step is implementing the agreement. A general meeting is recommended before implementation to refresh ideas and suggestions and allow for any additional relevant input. Further implementation meeting may include the following activities:

1. Discussion of a film, videotape, or cassette presentation;
2. Guest speaker (s);
3. A program featuring student projects from the resource room and regular classroom;
4. Appearances by former resource room students to discuss their experiences;
5. A transition meeting for students and their parents;
6. Meetings focusing on a particular theme;
7. A panel of parents to share their experiences and field questions;
8. A "Who's Who in Special Education" meeting to introduce parents to special education support staff;
9. Role playing of home/school scenarios followed by discussions.

At the who's who meeting, a special dinner might be planned to invite all participants. A panel involving the planner of the collaborative plan may want to conduct an informational meeting. Once the plan has been submitted, a question and answer period may follow, with the panel providing specific information to clear up any points. The panel's major objectives should be to clear up and questions relevant to the plan, and to offer other parents, teachers, and community individuals to share their concerns in a conducive and productive environment (Thompson, 1998; Casas, 1994; Davies, 1996; Clark, 1993).

A third step should be to evaluate the effectiveness of the plan by determining to what degree the stated goals and objectives were achieved. Several data sources may be employed to collect data relevant to the goals and objectives, such as questionnaires and surveys to teachers and parents, achievement test scores, amount and type of relevant services received, types of community resources used, and a summary of all collaboration efforts. Results from the evaluation may lead to changes and modification in the plan, if the stated goals and objectives were not effectively achieved. The evaluation may also indicate the need for additional training, and selection criteria for parents, educators, and community personnel. If evaluative results are negative, the negative aspects must be identified and corrected before implementation of the plan is continued.

MODEL PROGRAMS FOR IMPROVING COLLABORATION

Lewis and Morris (1998) reported on two successful programs involving parents working in the schools: The Charlotte-Mecklenburg, North Carolina and El Paso Public Schools. Koerner (1999) also reported on a successful collaborative program in Cobb County, Georgia. Thousands volunteered in these school districts to work in the schools, many of whom were parents. Volunteers served as teachers, mentors, lunch aides, lecturers, instructors in academic subjects, coaches and a variety of other services designed by the schools. Social events were also held to unify parents, teachers, and administrators. In addition, parental involvement included conducting mediation sessions and conflict resolution strategies, donation of goods and services, staffing the schools' administrative offices, and serving on advisory boards.

Another innovative approach to parental involvement is rating teachers. Some teachers may be threatened by this process, but research by Rich (1998) has shown that parental rating can introduce new concepts and ideas by providing innovative strategies to educate their children as well as providing the basis for on-going discussions relevant to curriculum modification. Parents rated teachers on the following:

1. Enjoying teaching;
2. Setting high expectations for children and assisting children in reaching them;
3. Demonstrating competency in the subject matter taught;
4. Creating a productive and safe environment for children to learn;

5. Effective strategies for dealing with behavior problems in a fair and just way;
6. Assigning meaningful homework assignments;
7. Understanding the principles of childhood development;
8. Using a variety of communicating tools to report students' progress and needs.

The issue of parental involvement in collaborative efforts in the school should not be imposed upon them by the school. Parents must feel competent in any involvement. They should have the right to choose not to be involved, when they feel that in their best interest their involvement will not benefit their children, or that they feel that they do not have the competencies to perform the assigned tasks. In essence, the degree of parental participation should be determined by the parents' needs and interests, not by some predetermined standards set by educators. A model for collaboration is presented to assist parents, educators, and the community in developing an effective collaborative plan. The aforementioned models project collaborative planning at its best.

A MODEL FOR PARENT-TEACHER COMMUNICATION

It has been projected through this chapter that a systematic plan was needed to develop a collaboration plan. The model appears to be one technique to develop a system-wide plan. The model is an attempt to visually be used in collaborative planning. According to Shea and Bauer (1991), their model is essentially a prescriptive-teaching methodology. Activities emphasize exclusively positive, human child-raising practice and behavior management techniques that recognize each parent and child as an individual with unique abilities, needs, and environment influences (see Table 4).

Implementation of the Shea and Bauer (1991) model can provide a format for providing a realistic model for collaboration and infusing, integrating, and respecting individual ideas. Additionally, the model will provide a mechanism whereby communication can be expedited and strategies included to improve interpersonal skills. Interpersonal skills training is needed by both teachers and parents. Since teachers are the professionals, they should be aware of interpersonal skills which will promote rather than retard communication in conferring with parents.

CONFERRING WITH PARENTS

Parents may request a conference concerning their children with disabilities for a variety of reasons. Teachers may feel apprehensive about the conference, but they should realize like themselves, parents also want their children to be successful, thus, viewing the conference as an opportunity to improve the educational opportunities for the children with disabilities. McLaughlin (1987) wrote that frequently teachers are not prepared in their training to conduct conferences and must learn on the job.

Parents also need to make preparations for attending a conference. According to Kines (1999), the following preparations are recommended:

1. Prepare a list of topics to discuss;
2. Involve the child if possible in a three way conference;
3. Be on time. It is unfair to keep others waiting; parents and teachers have busy schedules;
4. Come right to the point. Clarify pints to be discussed;
5. Ask about class participation of the child;
6. Request clarification on any issue not fully understood;
7. Ask to see child's work samples;
8. Talk about your child outside of school in order to inform the teacher of community and other out of school activities;
9. Stay within the time limit. If additional time is needed, schedule another meeting or a telephone conference;
10. Write a note of appreciation to the teacher, indicating the many positive things he or she has done to improve skills for the child. This note can indicate an agenda for the next meeting as well.

Table 4
THE PARENT-TEACHER COLLABORATION MODEL

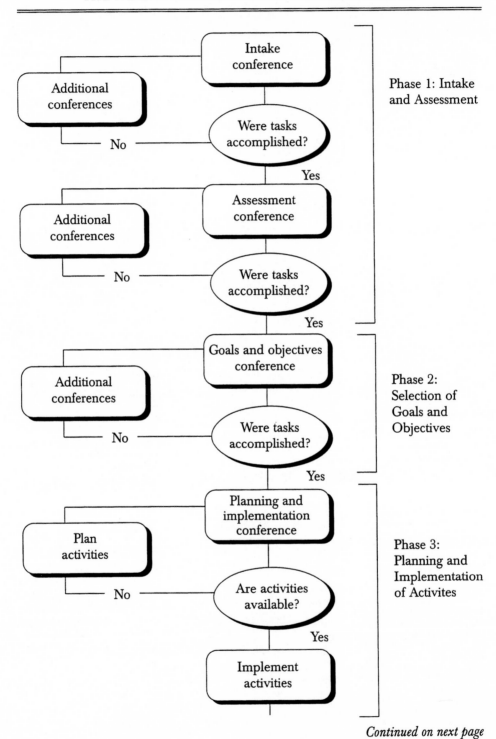

Continued on next page

Table 4–*Continued*

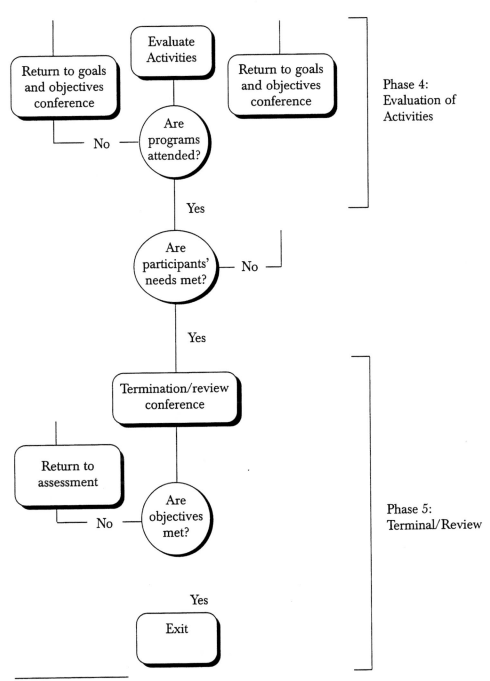

Reproduced by permission of author and publisher. For a detail and narrative description of the Model the reader is referred to: Thomas M. Shea and Anne M. Bauer (1991). *Parents and Teachers of Children with Exceptionalities: A Handbook for Collaboration.* Boston, MA: Allyn and Bacon.

Communication and collaboration are essential for teachers and parents, if children with disabilities are to profit sufficiently from their educational experiences. Some recommended strategies for teachers to improve communication and collaboration, according to Perl (1995), are:

1. Building Rapport—Establish the dignity and worth of the parent's contribution at the outset.
2. Listening—Learn to listen actively to the parent, be attentive to responses.
3. Empathy—Be aware of the nature and type of responses made by the parent; put yourself in the parent's place.
4. Reflecting Affect—Attempt to reflect how the parent feels. Show empathy at the appropraite times.
5. Clarifying Statements—Restate the question by saying do you mean or are you inferring a particular statement.

Parent-teacher conferences can serve useful purposes and provide invaluable information to improve the child's academic program (Fitton, 1996; Woeppel, 1990; Edwards, 1995; Whiteford, 1998; Wolf, 1998). Consequently, a positive approach must be taken by both parents and teachers. The first step is to improve the quality of communication. Carefully planned group and individual conferences are initial ways to improve communication. A successful group conference can set the tone for the year and build a strong rapport between teachers and parents.

THE GROUP CONFERENCE

Group conferences are designed to inform a large group about relevant educational and classroom issues. Group conferences are recommended over individual conferences when general issues are being discussed. Group conferences may serve as a general introduction meeting. Specific issues involving individual children should be reserved for small and individual conferences. Some general purposes of group conferences might include:

1. Parents become acquainted with the school's mission, the teachers, his or her instructional program, and materials and resources used in the instructional program.

2. Plans for involving the parents in the instructional program.
3. Plans for using or introducing advanced technology in the classroom.
4. A discussion on information relevant to a reporting procedure.
5. Addressing general questions posed by parents.
6. Establishing protocol and a schedule for future meetings.
7. Selecting a group leader.

A suggested format for conducting an initial group meeting or conference is reflected in Table 5.

Table 5

SUGGESTED FORMAT FOR CONDUCTING AN INITIAL GROUP MEETING/CONFERENCE

1. General Introduction
2. Purpose of the Meeting
3. Statement and Discussion of Objectives
4. Examples of How the Objectives Will Be Achieved
5. Parental Input on How Objectives Will Be Achieved
6. Discussing and Answering Any Questions from Parents Relevant to the Instructional Program.
7. Brainstorm on Various Ways Parents Can Assist to Promoting their Child's Achievement
8. Identify Specific Competencies of Parents and Elicit their Support in the Instructional Program
9. Conclude the Meeting with a Note of Appreciation to Parents for Attending the Meeting. Announce the Time for the Next Scheduled Meeting.

An initial group meeting, as outlined in Table 5, may have some negative consequences if the parents are not notified in a timely manner, individual needs are not met, an inconvenient time is set for some parents who are working, and inappropriate sites have been selected. The meeting should be accessible for parents with disabilities, transportation issues must be addressed, child care services should be available. Successful group meetings must stress the fact that parents are equal to teachers and have the right to serve on any committee to have their questions addressed in a professional manner (Rich, 1998; Perl, 1995; Steward, 1996).

SMALL GROUP CONFERENCES

Small group conferences can be productive if individuals in the group have similar interests and needs. Some of the same factors which operate in large groups also operate in small groups. Educators must decide on the group size. If the initial group becomes too large, additional small groups may be developed. There is no magic formula for determining the size of the group. Experiences, background, and competencies of the educator appears to be the best indicator for choosing the group size. Participants should be parents of children with similar problems and disabilities.

Parents participate in all aspect of the small group conference. They may serve as group leaders and resource individuals. Shea and Bauer (1991) summarized the roles and functions of small group leaders by indicating that planning lesson sequences is an important part of training, instructional, and information groups. Group leaders should be actively involved in all aspects of training. The major function of the group leader in small group conferences is to keep the group on task until the problem has been discussed and an acceptable solution has been found. It was commonly believed that since the group leader needed special competencies to lead groups, that the educator was the desired person. This belief is faulty; parents who have the skills may also serve as group leaders. It is incumbent upon the educator to assist in identifying the parent or parents who has/have the prerequisite skills to conduct the meeting. Once a parent leader is accepted, the educator should stay in the background and serve as a resource person only.

EFFECTIVE USE OF CONFERENCE INFORMATION

Collecting and gathering information is essential to conducting an effective instructional program for children with disabilities. Conferences are an excellent setting to collect these data. Data from the child's ecological environment should be collected and unified to give a complete profile of the child. Using this approach, the total needs and interests of the child can be successfully addressed in the instructional program. No one is better equipped than the parent in providing information on his or her child (Koerner, 1988; Graves, 1996).

Teachers must select those data sources which are relevant to her or his instructional program. Some suggested guidelines teachers may employ are:

1. Select and use information that will argument the instructional program.
2. Choose information that provides a clearer understanding of the student's disability.
3. Identify data sources that give insight into the child's outside interests.
4. Review information relevant to the family structure, family problems, and issues that may impact the instructional program, such as the child's relevant position in the family structure.
5. Evaluate any special devices or programs to which the child has been exposed.

A rationale should be given to the parent why information is needed. Most parents will freely provide information if they believe that the information provided will assist their children in any way. It is incumbent upon the teacher to maintain a professional view and ensure parents that all information will be used to assist the child in achieving the stated objectives. Personal comments and reaction to information provided by parents should be carefully monitored; in essence, teachers should refrain from making personal comments relevant to the cause or the blame for the information (Sullivan, 1998).

SUMMARY

Strategies for improving relationships for working with parents of children with disabilities will largely depend upon the nature and degree of disability, the parents' degree of participation, and the establishment of rapport between teachers and parents (Ysseldakes, Algozzine, & Thurlow, 1992; Friend & Bursuck, 1996). If rapport is not well established, it is highly unlikely that collaborative activities will be successful.

Educators may employ various ways of improving communication and collaboration with parents of children with disabilities. They may use workshops, conferences, and parent study groups. These approaches, other than parent-teacher conferences, are generally group-based; parents who have common problems can discuss them as well as have experts from various disciplines address the group. The principal sets the stage for parental involvement by working with school and community personnel. Joint planning and involvement between the school and parents cannot but help boost the parents' self-concept by incorporating them in the educational process.

As a means of strengthening the family in fulfilling its obligations to children with disabilities, the schools should provide educationally-related counseling and family services (Christenson et al., 1997). In cases of clear educational neglect, the schools, through qualified professional personnel, should make extraordinary arrangements for preventive and compensatory educational services. As a means of strengthening special education programs, parents of children with disabilities and organized community groups should be given a responsible part in educational policy formation and planning activities.

As outlined, assistance to parents is important in helping them resolve social and emotional difficulties affecting their children and to give advice regarding a plan for care as well as decisions concerning treatment and educational placement to ameliorate the disabling conditions. Diagnostic evaluation should further assist parents in accepting the fact that their children are disabled and provide information that will assist them in meeting the day-to-day problems that will arise. It is commonly recognized that no program will be completed successfully unless some parental involvement is sought and maintained. Cooperation between parents and school can aid the child greatly in his or her educational pursuits. Professional workers generally recognize that most parents have difficulty in accepting and adjusting to their children with disabilities. Consequently, without proper guidance, these factors can hamper the progress and development of children.

A first step for parents in accepting their children's disabilities is to recognize the basic problem and to seek ways to face the problems or disabilities with a positive approach. The difficulty of the problem is immense for most parents. Many will need individual as well as group counseling. The school can provide some counseling for parents if their problems are not too deep-rooted. More severe problems will have to be attended by mental health specialists. The salient point that school officials should keep centrally in mind is that some parents have received counseling and are ready to assist in educating their children; others are not so fortunate.

Collaborative activities can meet the needs of children with disabilities by integrating the services of both the home and school in all areas of human functioning. These activities may do much to improve culture, social, and physical problems associated with the children's disabilities. Parents must become an integral part of the collaborative efforts if they are to become successful. The following guidelines are offered as a means to improve the efforts:

1. Develop a plan to build trust and security among parents.
2. Involve parents in the school development plan; seek volunteers in all aspects of the plan to ensure that every parent contributes to the attainment of the goals and objectives.
3. Construct individual agreements with each parent so that the parent will have some responsibilities in meeting the stated goals, objectives, and IEP requirements.
4. Develop strategies for identifying, assessing, using, and evaluating community resources.

Collaborating with parents and working with families are major modifications and reforms in improving communication between the home and school. Much of the improvement in communication has come about due chiefly to state and federal legislation, parental rights groups, parent empowerment, and the schools' recognition of the value of parental input in educating children. The schools have become cognizant of the influence of poverty, race, ethnicity, family structure and transitions, parental age, and other factors which interact with children's development (Powell, 1995). Using the vast amount of research generated in the above areas, the schools have developed programs to strengthen parental behavior as well as revised programs to reflect cultural diversity.

REFERENCES

Ainsworth, F. (196). Parent education on family therapy: Does it matter which comes first? *Child Youth Care Forum, 25,* 101-110.

Booth, A., & Dunne, J. (Eds.). (1996). *Family-school links: How do they affect educational outcomes?* Hillsdale, NJ: Erlbaum.

Bryan, R. (1990). *Assessment of children with learning disabilities who appear to be socially incompetent.* Paper presented at the Annual Conference of the Council for Exceptional Children. Atlanta, GA.

Cairney, T. H., Ruge, J., Buchanan, J., Lowe, K., & Munsie, L. (1995). *Developing partnerships: The home, school, and community interface.* Canberra: Department of Employment, Education and Training.

Casas, M., & Furlong, M. J. (1994). School counselors as advocates for increased Hispanic parents participation in schools. In P. Pederson & J.C. Carey (Eds.), *Multi-cultural counseling in schools: A practical handbook.* Boston: Allyn and Bacon.

Cassidy, E. (1988). *Reaching and involving black parents of handicapped children in their child's education program.* Eric Document Reproduction Service. ED. 302982.

Christenson, S. et al. (1997). Parents and school psychologists' perspectives on parental involvement activities. *The School Psychology Review, 26,* 111-130.

Clark, R. M. (1993). *Family life and school activities.* Chicago: University of Chicago Press.

Cummings, J. (1984). *Bilingual and special education: Issues in assessment pedagogy.* San Diego, CA: College Hill Press.

Davies, D. (1996). Partnership for students success. *New Schools New Communities, 12* (13), 14-21.

Education Commission on the States. (1996a). *Listen, discuss, and act.* Denver, CO: ESC.

Epstein, J. L. (1991). Effects on student achievement of teacher practices of parental involvement. In S.Silvern (Ed.), *Literacy through family, community, and school intervention.,* Vol. 5. Greenwich, CT: JAI Press.

Epstein, J. L. (1995). School, family, community partnerships: Caring for the children we share. *Phi Delta Kappan, 77* (9), 701-712.

Fitton, L., & Gredler, G. R. (1996). Parental involvement in reading remediation with young children. *Psychology in the Schools, 33,* 325-332.

Floyd, L. (1998). Joining hands: A parental involvement program. *Urban Education, 33,* 123-135.

Friend, M., & Bursuck, W. (1996). *Including students with special needs.* Boston: Allyn and Bacon.

Giannetti, C. C., & Sagarese, M. M. (1997). *The roller-coaster years: Raising your child through the maddening yet magical middle school years.* New York: Broadway Books.

Giannetti, C. C., & Sagarese, M. M. (1998). Turning parents from critics to allies. *Educational Leadership, 55*(8), 40-42.

Gough, P. B. (1991). Tapping parent power. *Phi Delta Kappan, 22* (95), 339.

Griffith, J. (1998). The relationship of school structure and social environment to parental involvement in elementary schools. *Elementary School Journal, 99,* 53-80.

Graves, D. H. (1996). Parent meetings: Are you ready? How you prepare matters most in talking about a child's writing. *Instructor, 105,* 42-43.

Hatch, T. (1998). How community action contributes to achievement? *Educational Leadership, 55*(8), 16-19.

Kines, B. (1999). The parent connection. *Teaching K-8, 6*(4), 33.

Koerner, B. (1999, Jan). Parental power. *U.S. News and World Report.* Washington, DC.

Lewis, R., & Morris, J. (1998). Communities for children. *Educational Leadership, 55*(8), 34-36.

Lynch, E. W., & Stein, R. (1987). Parent participation by ethnicity: A comparison of Hispanic, Black, and Anglo families. *Exceptional Children, 54,* 105-111.

Marsh, D. (1999). *Yearbook: Preparing our schools for the 21st century.* Alexandria, VA: Association for Supervision and Curriculum Development.

Masten, A. C. (1994). Resilience in individual development: Successful adapttions despite risk and adversity. In M.C. Wang & E.W. Gordon (Eds.), *Educational resilence in inner city america.* Hillsdale, NJ: Erlbaum.

McLaughlin, C. S. (1987). *Parent-teacher conferencing.* Springfield, IL: Charles C Thomas.

Mills, D., & Bulach, S. (1996). *Behavior disordered students in collaborative/cooperative class: Does behavior improve?* Tampa, FL: Eric Document Reproduction Service No. ED 394224.

Penn, S. S., & Lee, R. M. (1992). *Home variables, parent-child activities, and academic achievement: A study of 1988 eight graders.* Paper presented at the Annual Meeting of the American Education Researcher Association, San Francisco.

Perl, J. (1995). Improving relationship skills for parent conferences. *Teaching Exceptional Children, 28* (1), 29-31.

Powell, D.R., & Diamond, K.E. (1995). Approaches to parent-teacher relationship in use early childhood programs during the twentieth century. *Journal of Education, 77* (3), 71-94.

Rich, D. (1998). What parents want from teachers. *Educational Leadership, 55* (8), 32-39.

Shea, T. M., & Bauer, A. M. (1991). *Parents and teachers of children with exceptionalities: A handbook for collaboration* (2nd ed.). Boston: Allyn and Bacon.

Stewart, C. (1996). The coach-parent meeting: The initial contact. *Strategies, 10,* 13-15.

Sullivan, P. (1998). The PTA'S national standards. *Educational Leadership, 55*(8), 43-44.

Taylor, G. R. (1999). Curriculum models and strategies for the disabled in inclusive classrooms. Springfield, IL: Charles C Thomas.

Thompson, S. (1998). Moving from publicity to engagement. *Educational Leadership, 55*(8), 54-57.

Wang, M. C., Haertel, G. D., & Walberg, H. J. (1993). Toward a knowledge base for school learning. *Review of Educational Research, 63* (3), 249-294.

Whiteford, T. (1998). Math for moms and dads. *Educational Leadership, 55*(8), 64-66.

Wilson, J. H. (1997). Communication, collaboration, caring family-center care. *Exceptional Parent, 28,* 61.

Woeppel, P. (1990). *Facilitating soical skills develooment in learning disabled and/or attention deficit disorder second to fifth grade children and parents.* Ed.D Practicum. Nova University.

Wolf, J. M. (1998). Just read. *Educational Leadership, 55*(8), 61-63.

Ysseldyke, J. E., Algozzine, B., & Thurlow, M. L. (1992). *Critical issues in special education* (2nd ed.). Boston: Houghton Mifflin.

Chapter 11

PARENTS' PERCEPTIONS OF PLACEMENT: INCLUSION OR SPECIAL EDUCATION

INTRODUCTION

Inclusive education has been defined in as many ways as there are attitudes toward this educational concept. For instance, Roach (1995) defined the term as serving students with a full range of abilities and disabilities in the general educational classroom, with appropriate in-class support. Written in the opinion of Brown, Schwarz, Udvari-Solmer, Kampschroer, Johnson, Jorgensen, and Greenwald (1991), inclusion is a way to implement the least restricted environment (LRE), however, the least restricted environment is not necessarily the regular education classroom. According to Bennett, Deluca, and Bruns (1997) and Scruggs and Mastropieri (1996), the concept of inclusion is the integration of students with disabilities into a heterogeneous classroom for the entire school day. This inclusive model is typically referred to as the Regular Education Initiative (REI).

It is the attitudes of those involved in, or affected by, inclusive models that define and determine the impact of this practice on the individuals who will be placed in this setting. For example, Berger (1995) asserted that the process of including individuals with special needs into the mainstream classroom has become a pressing issue among those in administration responsible for the education of these individuals.

A preponderance of literature attests to the fact that most children with disabilities should be placed in inclusive classrooms. This position has created some controversy regarding inclusive versus special class placement as noted by Baker, Wang, and Walberg (1994-1995); Zigmond et al. (1995); Borthwick-Duffy, et al. (1996); Fuchs and Fuchs

(1994); Rogers (1993); and Waldron and McLesky (1998). The common consensus of these researchers indicated that the concept of inclusion is an excellent idea; however, it may not work for all children all of the time.

Although the preponderance of research supports the concept of inclusion, some researchers question whether or not children with disabilities can receive an adequate education in a regular classroom setting (Fuchs, 1994; Borthworth-Duffy, Palmer, & Lane, 1996).

In summary, most of the research in opposition to inclusion states that inclusion will not work for children with disabilities due to the following:

1. Children with disabilities with serious problems tend to perform better in separate classes.
2. There is a need to preserve the continuum of specialized programs and placement options.
3. Children with disabilities enrolled in special classes performed as well as those in regular classes on curriculum-based measures.
4. Children with disabilities will interfere with the progress or regular students.
5. Placing children with disabilities in regular classes can lead to stigmatized labels.
6. Some regular students may begin to mimic inappropriate behaviors of some children with disabilities, thus affecting learning.
7. Some parents fear that services for their children with disabilities will not be available under inclusion.
8. Parents of nondisabled children fear that their children would be neglected in the classroom due to special attention required for children with disabilities.
9. Segregated schools are considered safe havens for some parents because they provide the specialized services needed for their children with disabilities.

VIEWS ON PLACEMENT

Teaching students with disabilities in inclusive settings is a multifaceted task that cannot be accomplished by just one person. Inclusive education happens when a team of mutually supportive players pledge to provide the best practices for a student with disabilities. Inclusive education focuses on a combination of best practices in education, including cooperative learning, peer tutoring, and community building in classrooms and schools. Teaching strategies for inclusive settings are synonymous with effective teaching strategies used in any area of education (Aefsky, 1995). Depending on the disability and level of student need, a team with unique but complementary skills should be consulted to guide, advocate for, and implement this student's educational program. More than any other element, the need for team effort to manage, deliver, and support a student's inclusive education is a drastic change for regular educators. Educators, must develop a plan to integrate the life-long goals and specific needs of students with disabilities within the context of the regular curriculum (Filbin, 1996).

According to Taylor (1999), collective research in support of inclusion is based upon:

1. Federal legislation in support of educating children with disabilities in regular classes. The reader is referred to Chapter 5, where a comprehensive review of the impact of federal legislation on inclusion is discussed.
2. Research findings tend to support that children with disabilities perform academically as well in inclusive classes as separate classes.
3. When provided with support, many children with disabilities are able to succeed in regular education classrooms.
4. The continuum of service model is not needed in inclusive settings; children with disabilities should be placed in regular classes on a full-time basis.
5. Children with disabilities will benefit from associating with their normal peers.
6. Inclusion will reduce labeling of children with disabilities.
7. Inclusion tend to increase interaction between students with disabilities and their nondisabled peers.

Advocates for full inclusion of children with disabilities indicate that it is their democratic right to be educated with their peers; integration of children with disabilities with nondisabled children enhances interpersonal skills. Other studies indicate that curricula in inclusive schools should be appropriate for different levels of disabilities and sensory acuity. There is no separate knowledge base for teaching students with disabilities. Teachers must be innovative and employ creative teaching strategies, such as learning centers, cooperative learning, concept teaching, directed teaching, and team teaching. Many adaptations and modifications will be needed in the instructional process, depending upon the amount and degree of disabling conditions present. To the extent possible, students with disabilities should be included in the learning process (Barry, 1995; Wang, Reynold, &

Walberg, 1995; Baker, Wang & Walberg, 1995; Staub & Peck, 1995; Johnson, Proctor & Corey, 1995).

Proponents of full inclusion believe that a one size fits all approach will be disastrous for children with disabilities; it is not only unrealistic but also unjust. To correct this injustice, according to Shanker (1995), public laws addressing inclusion will need to be rewritten to fund the cost of inclusion, provide adequate training for all teachers; to give equal weight to requests from parents and referrals from teachers, teachers must be totally involved in writing the IEP, and alternative arrangements should be made to temporarily place children with disabilities who are violent or disruptive in secure settings. The National Association of State Boards of Education voiced that many special education programs are superior to regular classrooms for some types of children with disabilities (Baker & Zigmond, 1990), and Fuchs, Fuchs, & Bishop (1992) and Fuchs & Fuchs (1995) reported that individualizing strategies employed in special classes are superior to one size fits all approach observed in many regular classrooms. They supported the view that separate is better for some children with disabilities, and to abolish special education placement in the name of full inclusion is to deprive many children with disabilities of an appropriate education.

EFFECTS OF RESEARCH AND LEGISLATION ON
PARENTAL PERCEPTION

The aforementioned research and the federal and state legislation discussed in Chapter 5, combine to have a significant impact on parental perceptions towards inclusion. Perceptions toward inclusion are multidimensional and differentiated by several factors (Anotonak & Larrivee, 1995; Larrivee, 1992; Schmelkin, 1981; Semmel, Abernathy, Butera, & Lesar, 1991; Wilczenski, 1992).

Integration of students with disabilities into the regular classroom and elimination of separate special education classrooms have been issues of major concerns to parents of children with disabilities well over several decades (Katsigannis, Conderman, & Franks, 1995; Sawyer, McLaughlin, & Wingler, 1994; Baker, Wang, & Walberg, 1994-1995; Borthwick-Duffy, Palmer, & Lane, 1996; Fuchs & Fuchs,

1994). A multitude of conditions and trends have attributed to the controversy.

Inclusion is an important issue because it affects virtually all stakeholders in education, including children with and without disabilities and their families, special and general education teachers, administrators, related services personnel, school staff, and the general public (Alper, Schloss, Etseheidt, & Macfarlane, 1995). Inclusion, a grassroots movement driven by parental dissatisfaction with the current delivery system and the conviction that all children should be educated together, has captured the attention of educators and the general public alike. According to Aefsky (1995), inclusion is turning the tables after 15 unsuccessful years of teaching children in a fragmented school society. Aefsky stated that we are asking professionals, teachers, administrators, and support staff to change their roles.

Effective inclusion necessitates the involvement of parents in the planning process. By way of review, parental involvement in IEPs is mandated by law. However, many parents of children with disabilities have concerns related to inclusion. They have voiced concern about their children in integrated classrooms. Some parents are sure that their children with disabilities are not receiving appropriate services; consequently, some have elected to have their children educated in segregated classrooms (Hobbs, Westling, 1998; Westling, 1996; Hanline & Halvorsen, 1989; McDonnel, 1987). Most of the studies relevant to parental perceptions on inclusion dealt with children with mild to moderate disabilities. A study conducted by Bothwick-Duffy and Palmer (1996) was designed to assess parental perceptions of children with severe disabilities. Parental reactions of these parents were similar to those of parents with children with mild to moderate disabilities. Regardless of the levels of disabilities, parents' views of inclusion are more related to well-defined goals and objectives, the personality traits of the teachers, attitudes of staff members toward disabilities, supportive services, competent personnel, innovated instructional strategies and delivery models, and resources and related services.

CRITICAL ISSUES TO BE CONSIDERED

When there is no consensus on goals or objectives, no type of placement for children with disabilities will be successful. An avoidance of clearly-stated goals and objectives cannot validate the success of any placement. If clearly beneficial objectives, unique for a particular disability, cannot be identified, then the issue should not be on placement, but rather developing the objectives and the support services needed to assist children with disabilities to reach their optimum levels of growth.

Teachers' Attitudes

Teachers' attitudes and expectations are critical elements in educating children with disabilities. A warm and sincere type of attitude is needed which reflects an understanding of the disability and the recognition that children with disabilities have the rights to be treated and educated as normal children are. This type of attitude should be demonstrated by all associated with treating and educating children with disabilities (Taylor, 1999).

Supportive Services

Supportive services and competent personnel are necessary in educating children with disabilities. Collaboration with community agencies should be sought and encouraged. Children with disabilities will need many support services outside the realm of the school. Competent and certified personnel are needed to educate and treat these children. High standards are needed for the selection of personnel. Before personnel are assigned to work with children with disabilities, the training, attitudes, and values should be precisely delineated.

Instructional Strategies

Instructional strategies employed in teaching children with disabilities should have been field tested and validated for the disability area. This will ensure that instructional strategies will assist in minimizing and reducing the disabling conditions of the children. Staff might be well trained to implement any type of instructional or delivery models.

Resources and Related Services

Resources and related services are needed to compliment the instructional program. Selection of resources and related services should be premised upon the assessed needs, interests, and abilities of children with disabilities. Personnel selecting the resources and providing the related services should be competent and certified in their selective disciplines.

Additional research is needed on parental perception toward educational placement of their children with disabilities. The research conducted has indicated that parents needed additional information on the critical issues listed; parents are more concerned about these critical issues rather than placement.

SUMMARY

Historically, the placement issue was discussed in the 1970s. The issue was whether handicapped children learned best in integrated or segregated classes. Most of the research indicate that prior to 1975, most handicapped children with mild disabilities were educated in integrated classes; those with severe to profound disabilities were educated in segregated classes. Federal legislation, P.L. 94-142 and amendments, changed this concept and gave all children with disabilities equality of education opportunities with the concept of the least restricted environment (LRE) which provided for all children with disabilities opportunities to be educated with their nondisabled peers. The law provided for both types of placements, integration and segregation. Assessment data used in completing the IEP are used to determine the LRE for students with disabilities. In comparing the research over the last two decades, data still support that most children with disabilities are placed in inclusive settings (Banerji & Daily, 1995; Edelman & Schattman, 1993; Sharpe, York, & Knight, 1994; Straub & Hunt, 1993; Robert & Mather, 1995; Zigmond, Jenkins, Fuchs, Deno, Baker, Jenkin & Couthino, 1995; Alper, 1995; Mills & Baluch, 1996).

Inclusion offers the nondisabled student an opportunity to develop an appreciation for the complexity of human characteristics as well as an appreciation for individual differences. Students who have not had these experiences may be surprised to learn that, for example, speech problems that accompany cerebral palsy do not necessarily indicate limited intelligence, cognitive impairment need not affect social development, and sensory impairment need not interfere with skill in motor activity. Additionally, students with disabilities may teach nondisabled learners to go beyond dysfunctional stereotypes. All students with behavior disorders are not aggressive, and students with learning disabilities can be highly capable in some academic areas. The advantages of inclusion have been well documented in the professional literature. In spite of the vast amount of support for inclusion, it is this author's view that inclusion is no panacea for educating all children with disabilities.

Parental perception supports the statement that inclusion is no panacea for educating all of their children. Parental perception vacillated greatly between inclusion and special education placement. The disability was not the chief reason why parents wanted their children in inclusive placements. Issues such as objectives, personnel, instructional strategies, delivery models, resources, and related services took precedent over placement.

REFERENCES

Aefsy, F. (1995). Inclusion confusion: *A guide to educating students with exceptional needs.* Thousand Oaks, CA: Corwin Press.

Alper, S., Schloss, P. J., Etscheidt, S. K., & MacFarlane, C. A. (1995). *Inclusion: Are we abandoning or helping students?* Thousand Oaks, CA: Crowin Press.

Anotonak, R. F., & Larrivee, B. (1995). Psychometric analysis and revisions of the opinions relative to mainstreaming scale. *Exceptional Children, 62,* 139-149.

Baker, E. T., Wang, M., & Walberg, H. G. (1995). The effects of inclusion on learning. *Educational Leadership, 59* (4) 33-35.

Baker, J., & Zigmond, N. (1990). *Full time mainstreaming: Are learning disabled students integrated into the instructional program?* Paper presented at the Annual Meeting of the American Educational Research Association. Boston: Eric Document Reproduction Service, No PD 320373.

Bannerji, M., & Dailey, R. (1995). A study of the effects of an inclusion model on students with specific learning disabilities. *Journal of Learning Disabilities, 28,* 511-522.

Barry, A. L. (1995). Easing into inclusion classrooms. *Educational Leadership, 52* (4), 4-6.

Bennett, R., Deluca, D., & Burns, D. (1997). Putting inclusion into practice. *Exceptional Children, 64* (1), 115-131.

Berger, S. (1995). Inclusion: A legal mandate: An educational dream. *Updating School Board Politics, 26* (4), 104.

Borthwick-Duffy, S. A., Palmer, D. S., & Lane, K. L. (1996). One size doesn't fit all: Full inclusion and individual differences. *Journal of Behavioral Education, 6,* 311-329.

Brown, L. P., Schwarz, A., Unvari-Solner, E. F., Kampshroer, F., Johnson, J. Jorgensen, J., & Greenwald, L. (1991). How much time should students with severe disabilities spend in regular classrooms and elsewhere? *Journal of the Association for Persons with Severe Disabilities, 16,* 39-47.

Filbin, J. et al. (1996). *Individualized learner outcomes: Infusing student needs into the regular education curriculum.* Eric Document Reproduction Services No. ED 400641.

Fuchs, D., & Fuchs, L. (1994). Inclusive schools movement and the radicalization of special education reform. *Exceptional Children, 60,* 294-309.

Fuchs, D., & Fuchs, L. (1995). Sometimes separate is better. *Educational Leadership, 50* (4), 22-26.

Fuchs, D., Fuchs, L., & Bishop, N. (1992). Teacher planning for students with learning disabilities: Differences between general and special education. *Learning Disabilities Research and Practice, 7,* 120-128.

Giangreco, M., Dennis, R., Cloninger, C., Edelman, S., & Schattman, R. (1993). I've counted JON: Transformation experiences of teachers educating students with disabilities. *Exceptional Children, 59,* 359-371.

Hanline, M. F., & Halvorsen, A. (1989). Parent perceptions of the integration transition process: Overcoming artificial barriers. *Exceptional Children, 55,* 487-492.

Hobbs, T., & Westling, D. L. (1998). Promoting successful inclusion. *Teaching Exceptional Children, 31* (1), 12-19.

Johnston, D., Proctor, W., & Carey, S. (1995). Not a way out: A way in. *Educational Leadership, 50* (4), 46-49.

Katsiyannis, A., Conderman, G., & Franks, D. L. (1995). State practices on inclusion: A national review. *Remedial and Special Education, 16,* 279-287.

Larrivee, B. (1992). Factors underlying regularly classroom teachers attitudes toward mainstreaming. *Psychology in the Schools, 19,* 374-379.

McDonnell, J. (1987). The integration of students with severe handicaps into regular public schools: An analysis of parent's perceptions of potential outcomes. *Education and Training in Mental Retardation, 22,* 98-111.

Roberts, R., & Mather, N. (1995). The return of students with learning disabilities to regular classrooms: A sellout? *Learning Disabilities Research and Practice, 10* (16), 46-58.

Roach, V. (1995). Beyond the rhetoric. *Phi Delta Kappan, 77,* 295-299.

Rogers, J. (1993). The inclusion revolution. *Research Bulletin, 1* (11), 106.

Sawyer, R., McLaughlin, M., & Winglee, M. (1994). Is integration of students with disabilities happening? An analysis of national data trends overtime. *Remedial and Special Education, 15,* 204-215.

Schmelkin, L. P. (1981). Teachers' and non-teachers' attitudes toward mainstreaming. *Exceptional Children, 48,* 42-27.

Scruggs, T. E., & Mostropieri, M. A. (1996). Teachers perceptions mainstreaming/inclusion: A research synthesis. *Exceptional Children, 63* (1), 59-74.

Semmel, M. I, Abernathy, T. V., Butera, G., & Lesar, S. (1991). Teacher perceptions of the regular education initiative. *Exceptional Children, 57*, 9-23.

Shanker, A. (1995). Full inclusion is neither force nor appropriate. *Educational Leadership, 50* (4), 18-21.

References

Sharpe, M. N., York, J. L., & Knight, J. C. (1994). Effects of inclusion on the academic performance of classmates without disabilities. *Remedial and Special Education, 15*, 281-287.

Staub, D., & Hunt, P. (1993). The effects of social interaction training on high school peer tutors of schoolmates with severe disabilities. *Exceptional Children, 60*, 41-57.

Staub, D., & Peck, C. (1995). What are the outcomes for non-disabled students? *Educational Leadership, 50*, (4), 36-39.

Taylor, G. R. (1999). *Curriculum models and strategies for educating individuals with disabilities in inclusive classrooms.* Springfield, IL: Charles C Thomas.

Waldron, N. L., & McLeskey, J. (1998). The effects of an inclusive school program on students with mild and severe learning disabilities. *Exceptional Children, 64* (3), 395-405.

Wang, M. C., Reynold, M. C., & Walberg, H. J. (1995). Serving students at the margins. *Educational Leadership, 50* (4), 12-17.

Wilczenski, F. L. (1992). Measuring attitudes toward inclusive education. *Psychology in the Schools, 29*, 306-312.

Zigmond, N., Jenkins, J., Fuchs, L., Fuchs, D., Baker, J., Jenkins, L., & Couthino, M. (1995). Special education in restricted schools: Finds from three multi-year students. *Phi Delta Kappan, 76*, 531-540.

Chapter 12

CONCLUSIONS AND IMPLICATIONS

OVERVIEW

From the very beginning, a child with a disability has an important place within the family. By being responsive to the child's needs for comfort, play, and love, a foundation for interactive social relationships is built. The drive for independence emerges as developmental skills grow. As the child tries to do more and more for himself/herself, he/she continues to depend on parents for guidance and support. Parental delight in the small accomplishments of a child can set expectations for larger successes.

Parents of children with disabilities, as well as all parents, have a tremendous influence and impact on setting appropriate models for developing social skills. As well as all skills, the developmental level of the child as well as developmental sequence must be considered in social skills training. Parents can contribute significantly to their children with disabilities' self-concept and control through appropriate modeling strategies (Dewitt, 1994; Di Martino, 1990).

In order for parents of children with disabilities to be effective change agents in promoting appropriate social skills development, early intervention in health care, counseling, housing, nutrition, education, and child-rearing practices, etc. must be improved. Early intervention and parental involvements are essential for preparing children to master social skill tasks successfully.

There has been strong support from the federal government to include the family in the early educational process of their children. Parental involvement permits children to successfully manipulate their environments. The federal government created guidelines for the educational community in developing and implementing a comprehensive, coordinated, multidisciplinary, interagency program of early intervention services for infants, toddlers, and their families (Gallager, 1989).

The role of parental participation in educating their children with disabilities, according to much of the research in the field, has shown limited participation between them and the school. This view has been interpreted to imply that parents simply had no interest in the education of their children (Lynch & Stein, 1987; Marion, 1981). Several factors may contribute to lack of parental participation and involvement. Many parents do not feel welcome in the schools. They believe that they have little to offer in educating their children.

Parents have played a major role during this century in improving special education services for children with disabilities. They have had support from national organizations. Refer to Appendix A for a list of major organizations in the United States supporting individuals with disabilities. These organizations operate on the state and local levels and were chiefly responsible for lobbying for federal and state legislation articulated in Chapter 5.

During the last three decades, federal and state legislation increased parental involvement in special education in several areas. The most significant legislation included the due process and impartial hearing procedures. These procedures were adequately addressed in Chapter 5. Safeguard procedures are basically the same in all states, with minor modifications. These procedures are mandated in federal and state legislation, designed to provide parents an opportunity to advance their case and to reduce the number of court cases filed by parents or school districts.

STRATEGIES FOR IMPROVING PARENTAL INVOLVEMENT

Recommended strategies for improving parental involvement in the schools have been indicated throughout this text. Much of the interest and increase in parental involvement may be attributed to P.L. 94-142 and its amendments. These legislative amendments have mandated parental participation in all aspects of the child's educational program, including assessment, IEP development, placement decisions, evaluation, follow-up, and transitional services. Some recommended strategies include:

1. **Rewarding parents.** Teachers need to recognize and reward parents for their involvement. Reinforcing parental efforts can make a significant impact in working with their children (Oswald & Sinah-Nirbay, 1992). Parents employ some of the same techniques that teachers use to reinforce their children. Social and academic growth of children with disabilities may be expedited through the use of reinforcement strategies. Teachers who create a positive atmosphere for communication and collaboration with parents increase the probability of the child's success in his or her academic pursuits.

2. **Modeling for parents.** Many parents are not trained in teaching strategies. Teachers can train interested parents through observation, demonstration, and modeling. Bandura (1977) has validated the importance of these techniques. Teachers should provide ample strategies for parents to imitate which, in their opinions, will improve instruction for children. Today, educators realize the importance of parental involvement and realize that cooperative efforts between teachers and parents benefits the children significantly.

3. **Conferences.** Both group and individual conferences have been found to be invaluable in improving collaboration between parents and teachers. Teachers may decide on the best type of conference needed to address the needs of the children. Some problems can be dealt with successfully in large groups, others in small groups. At any rate, confidentiality must be observed once the initial conference has been held; future conferences should be conducted on a regularly scheduled basis, agreed upon by both parent and teacher. Agenda for conferences should include items other than problems children are having. The author alluded to possible items in Chapters 6 and 10. Timing of conferences is of prime importance. Conferences must be held at a time which is conducive for parents to attend. The length of conferences must also be considered by teachers. Parents have other commitments and, to avoid conflicts, teachers should send out in advance conference schedules and agenda items. Advanced schedules should solicit parents' comments and suggestions. The final schedule should be modified to meet parental concerns. This approach will assist in assuring a sense of cooperation and openness between teachers and parents. Teachers and educators must be cognizant of the individual needs of parents and plan strategies based upon these needs. Various types of reinforcement strategies should be in placed to reinforce parental behaviors. The type of reinforcement or reward pro-

gram instituted should be conducted in concert with the individual needs of the parents.

Social and Academic Models

Changes are constantly occurring in early childhood. During this rapidly expanding period, children gain self-awareness and learn how to respond appropriately in different situations. Making sure that appropriate social and academic models are provided is a responsibility of parents. Children who are products of a stimulation and positive environment bring a sense of social maturity and independence to the learning environment. Research findings by Delgado-Gaitan (1991) and Salli (1991) support the above premise.

Not only are social skills important in academic areas, they are also related to socialization. Several behaviors are necessary in the socialization process, including the emergence of self-identity and self-concept. Social skills are developed through the interactions with family, school, and the community, but are none as important as the role of the parents.

Parents may stimulate social growth and development of their children in various ways. Some ways may include designing everyday situations for them to explore, providing activities to promote self-esteem and confidence, praising them frequently, providing support, and creating a healthy and safe environment, to name but a few positive activities needed for normal child development (Taylor, 1998).

Armstrong (1991) informed us that parental involvement is essential in assisting the school in developing appropriate social skills for disabled individuals. He concluded that involving parents in social skills homework makes transferring of social skills functional and realistic for children with disabilities. Parents may assist the schools in several ways. They may reinforce the social skills taught at home by providing practice and reinforcement for their children. They may also provide the school with valuable information concerning developmental issues, safety concerns, community resources, and demonstrations. Additionally, they may serve as resource individuals and accommodate the class on field trips.

Social changes are constantly occurring in early childhood. During this rapidly expanding period, children gain self-awareness and learn how to respond appropriately in different social situations. Making sure that appropriate social models are provided is a responsibility of parents. Children who are products of a stimulating and positive environment bring a sense of social maturity and independence to the learning environment. Research findings by Lareau (1987), Delgado-Gaitan (1991), and Salli (1991) support the above premise.

A recent *Reader's Digest* poll revealed that strong families give children an edge in school. Children who socially participate with family functions scored higher on tests than those who did not. The survey also revealed that strong family ties improved self-image and confidence in children. The family is the cornerstone for success in later life. Parent education appears to play a role in how well the student performs in school.

The quality of family life appears to be a significant factor in all of the groups. Children with disabilities from intact families performed better than those who lived only with their mothers. Strong family ties appear to reduce some of the anxiety faced by children with disabilities; children from families who attended houses of worship also scored higher on tests.

Creative and innovative ways relevant to family involvement must be experimented with to improve parental involvement, especially for parents of children with disabilities (Mansbach, 1993; Dalli, 1991). Factors such as (1) diverse school experiences, (2) diverse economic and time constraints, and (3) diverse linguistic and cultural practices all combine to inhibit parental involvement. Diversity should be recognized as a strength rather than a weakness. Parents need to feel that their cultural styles and languages are valued knowledge and that this knowledge is needed and welcomed in the school.

P.L. 94-142 and other federal amendments have mandated that parents be involved in planning education experiences of their children with disabilities IEP (Individualized Education Plan), which is part of P.L. 94-142 mandating parental involvement, from initial identification to placement of children with disabilities into educational settings. Additional mandates and ways of involving parents have been highlighted in Chapter 1. One recommended approach is to dialogue with parents in order to understand what they think can be done to improve involvement (Finders, 1994).

Unless the aforementioned strategies are adhered to, academic and social development of children with disabilities will be impeded. The combined cooperation of both school and home are needed if social skills training is to be effective. There is an urgent need to involve parents by making them aware of, as well as training them in the use of social skills techniques to implement at home. Cassidy (1988) reported that problems with scheduling, transportation, and the lack of knowledge of instructional programs and IEP procedures are partly responsible for poor parental participation.

The role of parents of children with disabilities in the school must supersede the mandates of P.L. 94-142 and its amendements. Parents must feel that they are welcome in the school and be given responsibilities concerned with planning, collaborating with teachers, and involvement in policy making. Parents should have an active role in planning and instructing their children and function as advocates for them if children are to profit significantly from their school experiences. Schools should experiment with various ways of improving parental participation, since they are the foremost educators of their children.

Innovated Practices

Over the last decades, the school has had a difficult time in establishing effective partnerships with parents. Much of the fragmentation has occurred because of noninvolvement, hostility, or parental indifference toward the school. Many schools serving parents of children with disabilities consider them a nuisance, unproductive, uneducated, lacking social grace, and not well informed on education and social issues. The relationship is further strained when parents internalize the negative behaviors displayed by the school and view the school as an unacceptable place which has no interest in them as individuals. There must be a total shift in the paradigm. The school must accept these parents and provide training and assistance in desired areas (Eisner, 1991; Barth, 1990).

The role of parental participation in education in general, and special education in particular, according to much of the research in the field, has shown limited participation. This view has been interpreted to imply that parents simply had no interest in the education of their children (Marion, 1981). Several factors may contribute to the lack of parental participation. Many parents do not feel welcome in the school. They believe that they have little to offer in educating their children. Cassidy (1991) reported that problems with scheduling, transportation, and knowledge of the Individualized Education Program (IEP) and special education procedures were partly responsible for poor parental participation. Other researchers implied that many parents, especially minority parents, disagreed with the present classification system. Many believed that their children were misplaced or rejected the diagnosis and assessment process used to place their children (Harry, 1992).

Parents provide the model of self-acceptance and the feeling that life is worthwhile. Also, parents who demonstrate a positive self-concept and high self-esteem treat their children with respect and acceptance and provide them with support and encouragement.

COMMUNITY AND PARENTAL INVOLVEMENT

It is commonly stated that no school program can be completely effective without the support of parents and the community. When parents and community become actively involved in the school program, the entire educational program for children with disabilities and their parents benefit. It becomes quite clear that when the school and community are genuinely interested in the welfare of the child and his or her parents, apathy and despair succumb to hope and self-fulfillment, which can do much to ease many of the emotional problems experienced. Further, improvement in communication can do much to eliminate the negativism that many parents have developed. This positive approach cannot but assist the child with a disability in his or her educational pursuits.

A desirable relationship in the community is one that is marked by a strong bond of understanding and cooperation between parents and school personnel. Parents should have a direct share in deciding what types of instruction appear to serve their children best. Parents should be welcome to make suggestions for the guidance of their children. Through various channels, the school should enlist the cooperation of parents and community agencies in designing and implementing educational programs for children with disabilities. In communities where educators work with parents and with religious, recreational, and social agencies in a constructive effort to help, the results are reflected in healthier personalities of boys and girls.

PARENTAL INVOLVEMENT 2000: SOME PROJECTIONS

Role of Institutions of Higher Education

In the next decade, it is projected that colleges and universities offering programs in teacher education will be required by national accreditation agencies to include skills and strategies for communicating and conferring with parents. It is commonly recognized that parents are the child's first teacher. Teachers must be trained to employ effective strategies to fully engage the parents in all educational activities, through collaborative efforts. Many teachers of individuals with disabilities have never experienced the presence of children with disabilities; consequently, they will need the expert opinions of parents in order to develop effective intervention techniques. Colleges and universities should include in their course offerings a course designed specifically for working with parents. Practicum and hands-ons experiences should be provided for students to work with parents and model behaviors demonstrated. One of the major purposes of this text is to provide strategies for training prospective special educators in colleges and universities.

Teacher training programs must prepare all teachers to work with parents of children with disabilities. Regular teachers must be exposed to the most innovative techniques in the field of special education, through increasing courses involving educating children with disabilities. The five-year teacher education program will take on significance if this view is supported.

Inclusion

P.L. 94-142 and its amendments specified major legislation dealing with parental involvement as outlined in Chapter 5. The major component of placement as related to parental involvement were addressed. The law stipulated that children with disabilities should be educated in the least restricted environment. Parents were to have an active role in deciding what constituted a least restricted environment. To many educators and parents, the least restricted environment implies placement in regular classrooms, inclusion, for all children with disabilities. On the other hand, there are opposing views (Bilken, 1989). Refer to Chapter 11 for the controversy concerning "inclusion." It is projected that by 2002, most children with mild to moderate disabilities will be contained in the regular classroom. For those children with severe to profound disabilities, full inclusion will be gradual over the next several decades; in some instances, some of these children may not be fully placed in inclusive classrooms. Parental perceptions and involvement will play a major role in the inclusion issue.

AN INTEGRATED APPROACH

In this text, attempts were made to provide educators and teacher with a blueprint to follow in involving parents effectively in the schools. Strategies were also provided for parents to implement in assisting teachers and educators in educating their children with disabilities. The fact that all segments of the community must collaborate in assisting parents in providing quality education for their children has also been stressed. A desirable relationship in the community is one which is marked by a strong bond of understanding and collaboration between parents, the school, and community agencies. Parental involvement should include all aspects of the child's school program as mandated by federal and state legislation.

REFERENCES

Armstrong, S. W., & McPherson, A. (1991). Homework as a critical component in social skills instruction. *Teaching Exceptional Children, 24,* 45-47.

Bandura, A. (1977). Social learning. Englewood Cliffs, NJ: Prentice-Hall.

Barth, R. (1990). *Improving schools from within.* San Francisco: Jossey-Bass.

Bilken, D. (1989). Making a difference ordinary. In W. Stainback & M. Forest (Eds.). *Educating all children in the mainstream of regular education.* Baltimore: Paul H. Brookes.

Cassidy, E. (1988). *Reaching and involving Black parents of handicapped children in their child's education program.* ED Document Reproduction Service. ERIC 302582.

Dalli, C. (1991). *Scripts for children's lives: What do parents and early childhood teachers contribute to children's understanding of events in their lives.* ERIC ED. 344664.

Delgado-Gaitan, C. (1991). Involving parents in the schools: A process of empowerment. *American Journal of Education, 100*, 20-46.

Dewitt, P. (1994). The crucial early years. *Time Magazine, 143*, (16), 68.

DiMartino, E. C. (1990). The remarkable social competence of young children. *International Journal of Early Childhood, 22*, 23-31.

Eisner, E. (1991). What really counts in school? *Educational Leadership, 10*, 17.

Erikson, E. H. (1995). Identity and life cycle. *Psychological Issues Monograph, 1*. New York: International Universities Press.

Finders, M., & Lewis, C. (1994). Why some parents don't come to school. *Educational Leadership, 51*, 50-54.

Gallagher, J. J. (1989). The impact of policies for handicapped children on future early education policy. *Phi Delta Kappan*, 121-124.

Harry, B. (1992). *Cultural diversity, families, and the special education system: Communication and empowerment.* New York: New York Teachers College Press.

Lareau, A. (1987). Social class differences in family-school relationships: The importance of cultural capital. *Sociology of Education, 60*, 73-85.

Lynch, E. W., & Stein, R. (1987). Parental participation by ethnicity: A comparison of Hispanic, Black, and Anglo families. *Exceptional Children, 54*, 105-111.

Mansbach, S. C. (1993). We must put family literacy on the national agenda. *Reading Today, 37*.

Marion, R. (1981). *Educators, parents, and exceptional children.* Rockville, MD: Aspen.

Oswald, D. P., & Sinah-Nirbay, N. (1992). Current research on social behavior. *Behavior Modification, 16*, 443-447.

Salli, C. (1991). *Scripts for children's lives: What do parents and early childhood teachers contribute to children's understanding of events in their lives.* ERIC. ED 344664.

APPENDICES

Appendix A

NATIONAL SERVICE ORGANIZATIONS

ACCENT on Information, Inc.
P.O. Box 700
Bloomington, IL 61701

Alexander Graham Bell Association
for the Deaf
3417 Volta Pl.
Washington, DC 20007

American Assoication on
Mental Deficiency
5101 Wisconsin Avenue, NW, Suite 405
Washington, DC 20016
    or
5201 Connecticut Avenue, NW
Washington, DC 20015

American Cleft Palate
Educational Foundation
Parent Liaison Committee
Louisana State University Medical Center
Dept. of Audiology & Speech Pathology
3755 Blair
Shreveport, LA 20852

American Coalition of Citizens
with Disabilites
1346 Connecticut Avenue, NW
Washington, DC 20036

American Council of the Blind
1155 15th Street, NW, Suite 720
Washington, DC 20036

American Foundation for the Blind
820 1st Street, NE, Suite 400
Washington, DC 20036
    or
11 Pen Plaza, Suite 300
New York, NY

American Lung Assoication
1740 Broadway, F114
New York, NY

American Printing House for the Blind
1839 Frantfort Avenue
P.O. Box 6085
Louisville, KY 40206

American Speech and Hearing
Association
9030 Old Georgetown Road
Bethesda, MD 20014

American Speech-Language-Hearing
Association
10801 Rockville Pike
Rockville, MD 20852

Association for Children and Adults
with Learning Disabilities
4156 Liberty Road
Pittsburgh, PA 15234

Association for the Education of the
Visually Handicapped
206 N. Washington Street
Alexandra, VA 22314

Association for the Learning Disabled
Box 69
Albany, NY 12201

Association for Retarded Citizens of the
United States
2501 Ave. J
Arlington, TX 76011

The Association for the Severely
Handicapped (TASH)
7010 Roosevelt Way NE
Seattle, WA 98115

Association of Learning Disabled Adults
P.O. Box 9722
Friendship Station
Washington, DC 20016

The Association of Handicapped Student
Service Programs in Post-Secondary
Education
Box 8256, University Station
Grand Forks, ND 58202

Boys Scouts of America, Scouting for the
Handicapped Division
P.O. Box 61030
Dallas/Ft. Worth Airport, TX 75261

Cancer Information Clearinghouse
National Cancer Institute
Bethesda, MD 20205

Candelighters Foundation
2025 Eye Street, NW, Suite 1011
Washington, DC 20006

Children's Division
American Humane Association
Box 1266
Denver, CO 80208

Coordinating Council for Handicapped
Children
220 South St., Room 412
Chicago, IL 60604

Cornelia de Lange Syndrome
Foundation
60 Dyer Avenue
Collinsville, CT 06022

Council for Exceptional Children
1920 Association Drive
Reston, VA 22091

Developmental Disabilities Office
U.S. Department of Health and Human
Services
200 Independence Avenue, SW. Room
338E
Washington, DC 20201

Developmental Disabilities Technical
Assistance System
Suite 300, NCNB Plaza
Chapel Hill, North Carolina 27514

Division of Developmental Disabilities
Department of Health, Education, and
Welfare
South Building, Room 3062
330 C Street, SW
Washington, DC 20201

Down Syndrome Congress
1640 W. Roosvelt Road, Room 156E
Chicago, IL 60608

Easter Seal Society
2023 West Ogden Avenue
Chicago, IL 60604

Epilepsy Foundation of America
4351 Garden City Drive, Suite 406
Landover, MD 20785
   or
18128 L Street, NW #406
Washington, DC 20001

Federation of the Handicapped
211 W. 14th Street
New York, NY 10011

Friederich's Ataxia Group in America
P.O. Box 11116
Oakland, CA 94611-0116

Girl Scouts of the U.S.A.
Services for Girls with Special Needs
830 Third Avenue
New York, NY 10022

Goodwill Industries of America
9200 Wisconsin Avenue
Washington, DC 20014

Helen Keller National Center for
Deaf/Blind Youth and Adults
111 Middle Neck Road
Sands Point, NY 11050

International Association for Parents
of the Deaf
814 Thayer Avenue
Silver Spring, MG 20910

March of Dimes
1275 Mamaroneck Avenue
White Plains, NY 10602

March of Dimes Birth Defects
Foundation
1275 Mamaroneck Avenue
White Plains, NT 10605

Mental Health Association
810 Seventh Avenue
New York, NY 10019

National Alliance for the Mentally Ill
1234 Massachusetts Avenue, NW
Washington, DC 20005

National Association for Visually
Handicapped
3201 Balboa Street
San Francisco, CA 94121

National Association of the Deaf
814 Thayer Avenue
Silver Spring, MD 20910

National Assoication for the Deaf/Blind
2703 Forest Oak Circle
Norman, OK 73071

National Association for Mental Health
10 Columbus Circle
New York, NY 10019

National Association for Retarded
Citizens
2709 Avenue E East, Box 6109
Arlington, TX 76011

National Association of the Physically
Handicapped
76 Elm Street
London, OH 43146
Appendix A Continued

National Institute of Mental Health
5600 Fishers Lane
Rockville, MD 20852

National Society for Autistic Children
169 Tampa Avenue
Albany, NY 12208

National Tuberous Sclerosis Association
P.O. Box 159
Laguna Beach, CA 92652

National United Cerebral Palsy
Chester Arthur Building, #141
425 Eye Street, NW
Washington, DC 20001

Orton Dyslexia Society
724 York Road
Baltimore, MD 21204

Osteogenesis Imperfecta Foundation
P.O. Box 428
Van Wert, OH 45891

Parents of Down Syndrome Children
11507 Yates Street
Silver Spring, MD 20922

People First National Inc
P.O. Box 12642
Salem, OR 97309

Pilot Parents
Mrs. Zelda Gorlick
102 Heathrow Drive
Downsview, Ontario, M3M, IX3
Canada

Prader-Willi Syndrome Association
5515 Malibu Drive
Edina, MN 55436

President's Committee on Employment
of the Handicapped
Washington, DC 20010

President's Committee on Mental
Retardation
Washington, DC 20201

Recording for the Blind, Inc
Anne T. McDonald Center
20 Roszel Road
Princeton, NJ 08544

Red Cross
17th and D Streets, NW
Washington, DC 20006

Special Education Programs
400 Sixth Street, Donohue Bldg.
Washington, DC 20016

Spina Bifida Association of America
343 S. Dearborn Dr., Suite 317
Chicago, IL 60604

Tourette Sundrome Association
41-02 Bell Blvd
Bayside, NY 11361

United Cerebral Palsy Association
66 E. 34th Street
New York, NY 10016

Appendix B

AN OVERVIEW OF THE INDIVIDUALS WITH DISABILITIES EDUCATION ACT
Amendments of 1997 (P.L. 105-17)
Bernadette Knoblauch

On June 4, 1997, President William J. Clinton signed the bill reauthorizing and amending the Individuals with Disabilities Education Act (IDEA). The bill became Public Law 105-17, the Individuals with Disabilities Education Act Amendments of 1997; it was the 17th law passed by the 105th Congress.

IDEA organized in four parts: Part A, General Provisions; Part B, Assistance for the Education of All Children with Disabilities (school age/preschool programs); Part C, Infants and Toddlers with Disabilities, and Part D, National Activities to Improve the Education of Children with Disabilities (support programs). P.L. 105-17 retains the major provisions of earlier federal laws in this area, including the assurance of a free appropriate public education (FAPE) in the least restrictive environment (LRE) and the guarantee of due process procedures. It also includes modifications to the law. Some of the changes that affect special education practice nationwide include:

- Participation of students with disabilities in state and district-wide assessment (testing) programs (including alternative assessment).
- Development and review of the individualized education program (IEP), including increased emphasis on participation of children and youth with disabilities in the general education teachers in developing the IEP.
- Enhanced parent participation in eligibility and placement decisions.
- Streamlined student evaluation/reevaluation requirements.
- Identification of transition service needs within a child's course of study beginning at age 14, the age at which transition services should begin.
- The availability of mediation services as a means of more easily resolving parent-school differences.
- Disciplinary procedures for students with disabilities, including allowances for an appropriate interim alternative educational setting.
- Allowing children ages 3-9 to be identified as developmentally delayed; previously it was ages 3-5.

153

Following are some of the highlights of the new law:

- Requires that parents be informed about the educational progress of their child at least as often as parents of nondisabled children.
- Specifies that a statement of transition services needs relating to course of study be included in the student's IEP beginning at age 14.
- Requires that instruction in and use of Braille be considered for students who are blind or visually impaired.
- Adds "orientation and mobility services" to the definition of related services.

Procedural Safeguards

In the area of procedural safeguards, IDEA 97:

- Requires more "user-friendly language" in delivering information to parents about their child's rights.
- Requires that parents be given access to all records relating to their child, not just those "relevant" records on the identification, evaluation, and educational placement of their child.
- Preserves existing procedural safeguards, such as due process and the right of the parents to recover reasonable attorneys' fees and costs if they prevail in administrative or judicial proceedings under IDEA. (But, in most cases, attorneys' fees cannot be reimbursed for IEP meetings.)
- Requires each state to establish a voluntary mediation process, with qualified impartial mediators who are knowledgeable about mediation techniques as well as special education laws and regulations.

Discipline

In the area of discipline, IDEA 97:

- Ensures that no student with a disability is denied ongoing educational services due to behavior. Schools must continue to provide educational services for students with disabilities whose suspension or expulsion constitutes a change in placement (usually more than 10 days in a school year).
- Gives schools the authority to remove students with disabilities to alternative settings for behavior related to drugs, guns, and other dangerous weapons for up to 45 days.
- Allows schools to place a student in an "interim alternative educational setting" (AES), another setting, or suspend a student for up to 10 days in a school year, in the same way students without disabilities are disciplined.
- Requires the IEP Team to conduct a "manifest determination" once a school decides to discipline a student with a disability. The IEP Team must determine within 10 calendar days after the school decides to discipline a student–whether the student's behavior is related to the disability. If the behavior is not related to the disability, the student maybe disciplined in the same way as a student without a disability, but special education and related services must continue.
- Permits school personnel to report crimes allegedly committed by students with disabilities to law enforcement authorities.

Outcomes and Standards

In the area of outcomes and standards, IDEA 97 requires states to:

- Include students with disabilities in state and district-wide testing programs, with accommodations when necessary.
- Establish performance goals for students with disabilities.

Evaluations and Curriculum

In the area of evaluations and IEPs, IDEA 97:

- Requires an explanation in the IEP, if necessary, of how state and district-wide assessments will be modified so that students with disabilities can participate in these assessments.
- Requires states to ensure that students with disabilities have access to the general education curriculum, and, if a student will not be participating in the general education program and extracurricular activities, an explanation in the student's IEP is required.
- Requires regular education teachers to be included on the IEP Team if the student is participating or might be participating in general education classes.
- Expressly requires that the IEP address positive behavioral intervention strategies, if appropriate.
- Requires state and local educational agencies to ensure that parents are members of any group that makes placement decisions.
- Streamline the reevaluation process, allowing parents and school districts to determine any areas in which reevaluation dates are not needed.
- Requires informed parental consent for all evaluations and reevaluations unless the school district can demonstrate that it has taken reasonable measures to obtain consent and the parent has failed to respond.

Early Intervention and Preschool Services

In the area of early intervention and preschool services, which is not Part C, IDEA 97:

- Requires that local school districts participate in a transition planning conference for toddlers with disabilities who are about to enter preschool.
- Explicitly calls for delivery of early intervention services in natural environments.
- Clarifies that the early intervention programs is payor of last resort.

Teacher Training and Preparation

In the area of teacher training and preparation, IDEA 97:
Creates a new system of grants to improve results for students with disabilities through system reform, emphasizing personnel training, and training for regular education teachers of early grades.

References

Bazelon Center for Mental Health (1998). A new idea: A parent's guide to the changes in special education law for children with disabilities. Washington, D.C.

The Council for Exceptional Children. 1998. *IDEA 97: Let's make it work*, Reston, VA.

New Jersey Developmental Disabilities Council, Fall 1997. *Common Ground.*

Illinois Assistive Technology Project. 1997. Tech Talk.

Individuals with Disabilities Education Act Amendments of 1997. (P.L. 105-17). 1997. 20 U.S.C. Chapter 33.

Kupper, L. (Ed.). 1998. The IDEA Amendments of 1997. *NICHCY New Digest*, 26 (Rev. ed.).

Appendix C

THE INDIVIDUALS WITH DISABILITIES
EDUCATION ACT (IDEA) AMENDMENTS OF 1997

What is the Individuals with Disabilities Act?

The Individuals with Disabilities Education Act, first enacted in 1975, guarantees the right to a free appropriate public education for all children with disabilities ages 3 through 21, inclusive. The law provides federal funding to assist states and local school systems to pay for special education and related services. In addition, IDEA contains provisions which help fund programs for infants and toddlers with disabilities and their families and a number of discretionary programs which help support the guarantees under the basic state grant program.

Why did the Congress change the law?

There were several motivations that resulted in the Congress doing a full review of this vital law. First, the authority for IDEA's so-called "discretionary programs" and the Early Intervention Program for Infants and Toddlers had expired, and they needed to be reauthorized. Second, the law had never been comprehensively reviewed in its twenty-two year history. Third, society and schools in general have changed substantially over the past two decades, resulting in new and difficult challenges and pressures to our nation's schools. Discipline and school safety, serious funding crises and the lack of student achievement and the accountability of schools and their leaders have troubled our country for some time. Special education has not escaped these problems.

Fourth, special education has suffered from an escalating backlash from many parents of children without disabilities, many school authorities, and from the media. Fifth, even some parents of special education students were disgruntled with the implementation of IDEA as it related to their child. For example, many are unhappy with the inability of their child to be educated with their nondisabled peers. Finally, special education has been severely criticized by the very professionals who are responsible to implement IDEA. Many school boards, administrators, and teachers criticized the law from several perspectives.

What are they key aspects of the revised IDEA?

President Clinton signed the 19997 IDEA amendments into law (P.L. 105-17) on June 4, 1997. The revised law represents a fair and balanced compromise, leaving no party involved in the legislation process completely satisfied. From The Arc's perspective, there are many improvements to the law and several serious concerns.

Key positives in IDEA include:

- Cessation of education services is prohibited.
- Educational improvement is emphasized.
- Parental participation in decision-making is improved.
- Individualized educational programs are strengthened.
- Dispute resolution through mediation is encouraged.
- Funding formulas for schools are revised.
- Special purpose programs are revamped.

Potential concerns include:

- Limitations on attorney fees reimbursement for parents.
- Expanded and stricter discipline provisions.
- Potential misinterpretations and misapplication of the new law by school authorities.

How will the new law help parents better participate in their child's education?

First, it is critical for parents to know that the basic guarantee of a free appropriate public education (FAPE) and the due process procedures to protect this guarantee remain in the law.

One major improvement in the law now guarantees that parents will be part of any decision made about where the child will receive his/her education. Allowing parents to participate in the placement decision will help those who seek to see their child included in classes and programs with nondisabled children.

Schools must now provide parents of special education students with regular reports on student progress, at least as often as parents of nondisabled children receive them, usually through report cards.

IDEA also provides funding for Parent Training Centers to help parents be educated and receive training and technical assistance on the new law. School authorities are also now required, where necessary and when feasible, to communicate directly with parents about parents' rights in simple terms and using the native language of the family.

What new provisions in the law will help students with disabilities do better in school?

Many new parts of IDEA aim to improve results for students with disabilities.

These include:

- emphasis on access to the general education curriculum.
- a statement of transition service needs of the child beginning at age 14 and beginning at age 16 and younger, if needed, a statement of transition services included in the child's Individualized Education Program.
- school officials having to give an explanation in the child's Individualized Education Program of the extent that child will not be educated with non-disabled children; including students with disabilities in all state and district-wide assessments.
- providing alternative assessments for those students who cannot reasonably be expected to participate in general assessments.
- eliminating unnecessary testing and evaluations and make re-Evaluations more instructionally relevant and
- require appropriate behavior interventions to prevent and address disciplinary concerns.

How does IDEA address those concerns expressed by school authorities?

The revised IDEA contains numerous provisions to help school officials meet their special education responsibilities. In regard to funding, the law revises the funding formula. Eventually, the child count system in effect for twenty years will be replaced by a formula that distributes "new" money based 85 percent on the general population and 15 percent on a poverty factor. This formula will be in effect once the IDEA State Grant Program is funded at a level exceeding just over $4.9 billion (currently funded at $3.1 billion).

Local school systems would also get relief when funding exceeds $4.1 billion for the IDEA state grant program. When that appropriation is reached, a school system can use up to 20 percent of its Part B funding that exceeds the amount it received under Part B the previous year for other purposes. The new IDEA also established stronger provisions for interagency agreements with other state agencies to help with the cost of special education.

In addition to fiscal issues, schools will be helped with reductions in paperwork burdens, limitations on parents' access to certain attorney's fees even though parents prevail in court, regular education teachers involved with a special education child will now be included in IEP decisions, and by stricter discipline measures.

How does IDEA promote safer, better disciplined students?

IDEA substantially changes the law regarding discipline. School officials will still be able to discipline any student with a disability for up to 10 school days when students violate school rules. Very importantly, students will return to their original placements (unless the parents and school officials agree otherwise) in most disciplinary matters.

School officials will now be able to place students with disabilities in an interim alternative educational setting for the same amount of time a child without disability would be subject to discipline, but no more than up to 45 school days if students:

- bring a weapon to school or to a school function.
- knowingly possess use, or sell illegal drugs in school or at a school function or
- a hearing officer may order a change in placement for a child with a disability to an interim alternative educational setting for not more than 45 days if the hearing officer finds that the student is substantially likely to injure him or her self or others.

Before a removal of more than 10 school days, a "manifestation determination" must be made to ascertain if the students' actions are related to their disability. If the action is determined to be unrelated to the disability, students with disabilities may be discipline the same way students without disabilities are disciplined. In making the manifestation determination, the hearing officer must also consider whether the child's disability impaired h is/her ability to (1) understand the impact and consequences of the behavior and (2) control the behavior. However, no student with a disability may have his/her education ceased. Free appropriate public education must be provided during any removal beyond ten school days.

Who decides if a student is "substantially likely to injure" and what standard is used to make that determination?

A hearing officer makes the decision, using a standard higher than the one previously used by the courts in such cases. Local school authorities must prove substantial likelihood of injury by "substantial evidence." Substantial evidence" is further defined as "beyond a preponderance of evidence," a higher standard than Courts used, using the Honig Supreme Court decision as the basis of decisions. In addition, the hearing officer must consider the appropriateness of the child's current placement and whether school officials made reasonable efforts to minimize the risk of injury.

In the alternative placement, the child must continue to participate in the general curriculum and continue to receive services and modifications, including those in his/her current IEP that will enable the child to meet the IEP goals and to receive services that are designed to address the behavior that led to the placement of the child in that setting.

How will "disruptive" behavior be addressed in the law?

Although the issue of "disruptive" students was given serious consideration during the debate over the reauthorization of IDEA, the IDEA amendments of 1997 contain no mention of "disruptive" students. The ARC was adamantly opposed to any such provision.

There are a number of provisions, however, in the IEP process aimed at addressing the behavior of students with disabilities. For example, when a child's behavior impedes his or her learning or that of other students, the IEP team shall consider, when appropriate, strategies, including positive behavioral interventions, strategies, and supports, to address that behavior.

How does the law help parents and school systems resolve disputes?

For the first time, IDEA requires each state to put in place and find a mediation system. Mediation is voluntary for both parents and the schools. Each mediator must be qualified and impartial. Mediation cannot be used to deny or delay a parent's right to a due process hearing. Parents who decide not to enter mediation, however, may be counseled about the utility of mediation in resolving disputes and encouraged to use it by a disinterested party. Attorney's fees need not be awarded for mediation at the discretion of the state for a mediation that is conducted prior to filing a due process complaint by the parent.

Can parents still be reimbursed for the costs of attorney's fees if they prevail in due process?

Yes, but with certain new limits. For example, attorney's fees are not reimbursable for the use of an attorney at the IEP meeting, unless the IEP meeting is the result of an "administrative proceeding or judicial action." As stated earlier, attorney's fees cannot be awarded for mediation prior to filing a due process complaint unless the state allows for such reimbursement.

Courts can reduce fees if the parents' lawyer did not provide the school district with appropriate information as required by law. Parents are also required, directly or through their attorney, to notify the school system of their concerns prior to filing a due process action if they later wish to claim fees. Included in the information parents must provide to the school system are the child's name, the child's address, and the school of the student, a description of the nature of the problem with the child's education, and if known, a proposed resolution.

Attorney's fees can also be reduced if the Court concludes that the parents unreasonably protracted a final resolution of the situation. Conversely, fees cannot be reduced if the Court finds that the school system unreasonably protracted matters.

How does IDEA now deal with the transfer of parental rights?

Essentially, the new law allows states to permit the child with a disability to obtain all relevant rights at the age of majority, with two exceptions. First, the child will not obtain such rights if he/she has been found incompetent under state law. Second, if the child has not been deemed incompetent but is unable to provide informed consent in decision-making, states may establish a procedural less burdensome than a competency hearing to allow parents to retain the rights.

Are there any changes to Part H, the Early Intervention State Grant for Infants and Toddlers?

Part H will now be known as Part C, beginning on July 1, 1998. Although the ARC and other disability groups sought a permanent authority for Part H, the Congress reauthorized the new Part C for five years. A number of find tuning provisions were added to Part C. They include:

- the addition of a new definition of "at risk infant and toddler" to mean a child under three years of age who would be at risk of experiencing a substantial developmental delay if early intervention services were not provided.
- a number of new provisions altering the statewide system requirements.
- a number of new provisions to the Individualized Family Service Program; including a provision requiring the service agency to justify the extent, if any, that services will not be provided in a natural enviornment (e.g., the family home) and
- new membership requirements and role revision for the State Interagency Coordination Council.

What happens to the IDEA discretionary programs?

The new law makes massive changes to the IDEA discretionary programs. First and foremost, the number of programs decreases from fourteen to three. One represents a new Federal initiative while the other two merge and consolidate existing programs. These became Part D of the law.

The new program established a competitive grant program, called the State Program Improvement Grants, aimed at reforming special education programs. Seventy-five percent of the funds (50 percent under certain conditions) will address personnel preparation, particularly in-service training. States that receive grants will receive from half a million to two million dollars annually. The grants emphasize partnerships with local school systems and other state agencies and disability groups, including parents.

The other two programs consolidate existing discretionary programs. The coordinated research and personnel preparation section will deal with issues such as:

- early childhood education
- serious emotional disturbance
- personnel development
- severe disabilities
- innovation and development
- transition services

The coordinated technical assistance, support, and dissemination program will embrace the following activities:

- parent training
- information clearinghouse
- technology
- regional resource centers

Part D programs are authorized for five years, through FT 2002.

The Part I Family Support Program is reauthorized, by only until October 1, 1998. This unfunded program will need to find a home in another law. The ARC intends to seek reauthorization of this as yet unfunded program in legislation related to programs housed within the Department of Health and Human Services.

Are all the provisions of IDEA effective upon enactment?

No, there are a number of dates where specific components of IDEA will take effect. Some of the more important implementation dates are:

- October 1, 1997 Part D Discretionary Programs
- July 1, 1998 IEP revisions, Part C Early Intervention
- July 1, 2001 Alternative assessment for those students who cannot participate in regular assessments.

Most of the key provisions in the IDEA State Grant Program will be in effect for the school year that starts on or about September 1, 1997.

Now that the legislation is law, what are the relevant implementation issues?

The work of the Congress is not done. Attention new shifts to the FY 1998 appropriations process. Funding for IDEA ins contained in the Departments of Labor, Health and Human Services and Education appropriations bill.

Since the new fiscal year begins on October 1, 1997, the Congress has until then to appropriate funding for the revamped IDEA. Republican leaders in the House and the Senate have pledged to secure major funding increases ($1 billion) for IDEA. The ARC will work to support increased funding for all components of IDEA, the Part B State Grant Program, the Preschool Program, Part C Early Intervention, and Part D Discretionary Programs.

Much attention now shifts to the U.S. Department of Education, which must develop regulations to implement the new law. Preliminary plans call for the Department to promulgate proposed rules in the Federal Register by the end of September or early October. A 90-day public comment period follows. Plans also call for six regional hearings to be held on the proposed regulations. Final regulations are scheduled to be published by the end of April, 1998. The Arc must be fully prepared to comment on the proposed rules this fall.

The Department of Education will also undertaken major training and technical assistance activities to inform all affected parties about the changes to IDEA. It is vital that parents take part in these sessions to learn about the new law.

What can leaders of the Arc do to make sure that the rights of students with mental retardation and parents remain guaranteed and that educational outcomes for students with disabilities meet the promise of the new IDEA?

Almost all aspects of the new fall to state and local educational agencies to implement. It is vital that leaders of the ARC at the state and local levels first learn about new law and then work closely with state and local school authorities as they set policy to implement the law. The ARC at all levels should participate in training and other activities aimed at full and accurate implementation of the law.

The ARC at all levels has monitored special education implementation for more than two decades. Enactment of the IDEA amendments of 1997 requires a redoubling of monitoring efforts since the promise of this law will not be realized in many communities unless strong monitoring takes place.

How can the Arc further advocate for inclusion for students with mental retardation under the new law?

For decades, the ARC has demonstrated and decried the lack of inclusion of students with mental retardation in regular education settings. New tools are now available to help parents and students achieve this goal. Parents are now part of the placement decision-making process. School systems must now give an explanation in the IEP of the extent to which a child is not included with nondisabled peers. These two provisions can give those parents who seek to have their child in regular classes unprecedented leverage. Parents must be informed and trained about these important provisions and then use them to secure appropriate educational programs for their children.

Are there issues that should cause serious concern for parents?

Yes. The ARC is especially concerned about potential abuse by school officials of the new "substantially likely to injure" provision. This provision could be used inappropriately by those teachers and administrators who don't want students with mental retardation in regular educational settings. Although the Congress set a high standard for school authorities to prove a student would be "substantially likely to injure," this provision will require close monitoring by the Federal and state governments, as well as parents and advocates.

Numerous other provisions could be adversely manipulated by school officials to the detriment of students. Again, knowledgeable parents and advocates must step in and be heard when such abuses arise.

Where can I get more information about the new IDEA?

Many entities, governmental and public, are now developing materials to explain the new law. Check with the Parent Training and Information Center in your state. Their information will be slanted for use by parents.

Contact your state chapter of the ARC for the location of your PTI. The U.S. Office of Special Education Programs is also developing materials. They can be contacted by writing to OSEP, Switzer Building, 330 C Street, Washington, D.C. 20202 or by calling (202) 205-5507.

The ARC's Governmental Affairs Office is always available to assist you. Contact them by writing to 1730 K Street, NW, Suite 1212, Washington, D.C. 20006, or by calling (202) 785-3388 or e-mail at arcga@radix.net. The Governmental Affairs Office has also sent a package of preliminary materials developed by several sources about IDEA to all state chapters of the ARC, as well as a copy of the law and a useful video on the new law.

Note: This document was reviewed for consistency with the Individuals with Disabilities Education Act (P.L.. 105-17) by the United States Office of Special Education Programs.

*This Q&A has been prepared to provide an early introduction of the 1997 Amendments to IDEA. It presents aspects of the law's development, describes changes to the law and discusses implementation issues. It will be most helpful when read in conjunction with "The New IDEA: Knowing your rights" video.

Appendix D

READINGS ON THE IDEA AMENDMENTS
OF 1997

Bock, S.J. et al. (1998). Suspension and Expulsion: Effective Management for Students? Intervention in School and Clinic, 34(1), 50-52.
This article provides a brief review of legal procedures that schools have available under the Individuals with Disabilities Education Act (IDEA) Amendments of 1997, and discuss problems with using suspension and explosion, including recidivism, increased dropout rates, overrepresentation of minorities receiving suspeension or expulsion, and indiscriminate suspension and expulsion.

Bureau of Indian Affairs, Dept. of Interior. Washington, DC. (1997). Educational Rights of Parents under Provisions of the Individuals with Disabilities Education Act Including the Amendments of 1997 (Special Education). 24p. ED416661.
This pamphlet describes the educational rights of parents provided under provisions of the IDEA, including the amendments of 1997. It discusses rights in the following areas: free appropriate public education; prior notice to parents; parental consent; independent educational evaluations; educational surrogate parents; students records; mediation; discipline; state complaint procedures; impartial due process hearings; and private school placement. The pamphlet ends with a summary of parents' rights.

IDEA 1997: Let's Make It Work (1998). Council for Exceptional Children, 1920 Association Dr., Reston, VA 20191. 94p.
This document explains provisions of the 1997 amendments to IDEA (Public Law 105-17) and is divided into 16 topics, most of which address specific sections of the law. Topics include parental involvement; developmental delay; cultural diversity; evaluation and reevaluation; the individualized education program (IEP); related services and technology; early childhood; procedural safeguards; mediation; behavior and discipline; state and local fiscal management responsibilities; private school placements; performance goals, indicators, and assessments; and national support programs. Two additional sections provide a summary of IDEA, an index of topics located in the legislation, and a list of general resources for IDEA.

Johns, B.H. (1998). What the New Individuals with Disabilities Education Act (IDEA) Means for Students Who Exhibit Aggressive or Violent Behavior. (Theme Issue: Aggression and Violence in the Schools–What Teachers Can Do) Preventing School Failure, 42(3), 102-05.
This article outlines new provisions in the reauthorized Individuals with Disabilities Education Act that benefit children with behavior or emontional disorders. Provisions that focus on keeping students in school, accurate assessment of student behavior, positive behavioral interventions, and children who bring weapons or drugs to school are discusses.

Landau, J.K., (1988). Statewide Assessment: Policy Issues, Questions, and Strategies. PEER Policy Paper. 7p. (ED number to be assigned)
This policy paper provides a list of questions and associated strategies that parents and parent organizations can address in an effort to ensure that statewide assessment systems fully and fairly include students with disabilities as required by the 1997 IDEA and other federal laws. Introductory material notes that purposes of these large-scale assessments and the relation of statewide assessment programs to education reform initiatives. Suggested questions address the following issues: type of assessment used, use of "off the shelf" or contracted assessments, the process for developing the assessment, the consequences for students of the statewide assessments, inclusion of all students with disabilities in the assessment, responsibility for determining if a student with disabilities needs accommodations to participate in the assessment, types of accommodations available to students with disabilities, how test results are to be used, and how test scores of students with disabilities will be reported. Among seven strategies recommended to parents are the following: obtai copies of state's education reform and assessment legislation, regulations, and policy documents; identify who makes policy decisions about participation of students with disabilities,; and get involved in the decision-making process.

McConnell, M.E. et al. (1998). Functional Assessment: A Systematic Process for Assessment and Intervention in General and Special Education Classrooms. Intervention in School and Clinic, (34), 1, 10-20.
This article describes a 10-step process that educators can use when conducting functional assessments and developing Behavioral Intervention Plans required under the IDEA 1997 for students with disabilites with behavior problems.

Manasevit, L.M. et al. (1997). Opportunities and Challenges: An Administrator's Guide to the New IDEA. 212p. ED415649.
This manual is designed to help state and local administrators, school board members, and other education advocates understand the complex requirements of the newly authorized IDEA. This manual provides step-by-step instruction on IDEA's administrative and procedural requirements. It discusses some of the problems with the old act and highlights the nature of and reasons for the changes. The manual identifies new questions arising from the reauthorized IDEA and discusses potential outcomes under the new statue. If offers insight into

the interpretatons likely to follow in regulatons or the courts and provides practical guidance for understanding IDEA. The manual focuses primarily on the requirements of Part B, the state grant program which provides financial assistance for educating children with disabilities. Individual chapters discuss the changes to state and local planning requirements; identification, evaluation, and placement of children with disabilities; the IEP process; discipline; procedural safeguards; and fiscal obligations. The manual also gives an overview of the program that provides assistance for infants and toddlers with disabilities, known as Part C of the Act.

National Information Center for Children and Youth with Disabilities (NICHCY), Washington, DC. (1998). The IDEA Amendments of 1997. Revised Edition. 39p (ED number to be assigned)
This news digest summarizes the reauthorized IDEA with emphasis on changes in the new law. These changes include participation of children and youth with disabilities in state and district-wide assessment programs; the way in which evaluations are conducted; parent participation in eligibility and placement decisions; development and review of the (IEP); transition planning; voluntary mediation as a means of resolving parent-school controversies; and discipline of children with disabilities. A side-by-side analysis of how the IDEA has been changed is included.

O'Leary, E. (1998). Transition: Terms and Concepts. 15p. ED419330.
This paper provides explanations and case examples of some terms and concepts related to transition of students with disabilities under the 1997 amendments to IDEA. Explanations and examples focus on the concepts of "statement of transition service needs" and "statement of needed transition services." The statement of transition service needs focuses on the student's course of study and other educational experiences and is required on an IEP for every student who is 14 years of age and older. The statement of needed transition services is a long-range 2-to-4 year plan for adult life and is required for every student with an IEP who is 16 years of age and older (younger, if appropriate). This statement must include long-range, post-school planning in the areas of instruction, employment, community experiences, post school adult living, and related services. Also addressed is involvement of other agencies in cooperation with the schools. A sample form for meeting transition requirements includes space for specifying desired post-school outcomes, the present level of educational performance, the statement of transition service needs, and the statement of needed transition services (presented in a matrix form showing specific services, activities/strategies, agency/responsibilities, and who will provice and/or pay).

Palmer, S. (1997). Early Intervention Services for Children Birth through Age 2 Enacted by P.L. 105-17 (IDEA 97). 4p. ED416647.
This fact sheet uses a question-and-answer format to summarize early intervention services for children (birth through age 2) provided by Part C of the Individuals

with Disabilities Edcation Act of 1997 (Public Law 105-17). Questions and answers address the following topics: the purpose of Part C (early identification and intervention with infants and toddlers); eligibility for services under Part C (children under age 3 with developmental delay or diagnosed conditions); services mandated to eligible children and their families; the Individualized Family Service Plan; procedural safeguards under Part C; the role of the state and federal governments in providing services; services that each state must provide (such as a comprehensive child and referral system); and paying for early intervention services.

Appendix E

PARENT DUE PROCESS CHECKLIST

• The right to examine all school records concerning your child.

• The right to obtain an independent evaluation.

• The right to determine whether the hearing will be closed or open to the public.

• The right to advice of counsel and representation by counsel at the hearing.

• The right to bring your child to the hearing.

• The right to keep your child in his/her current educational placement until all due process hearing appeals have been completed.

• The right to written notification about the hearing in the primary language or mode of communication of the parent.

• The right to present evidence and testimony.

• The right to prohibit the introduction of any evidence which has not been disclosed to parents at least five days prior to the hearing.

• The right to cross-examine and challenge all testimony presented during the hearing.

• The right to receive a verbatim transcript of the hearing, at reasonable cost.

• The right to appeal the decision of the hearing officer or hearing panel.

Appendix F

THE MANIFESTATION DETERMINATION REVIEW: WAS THE CHILD'S BEHAVIOR A MANIFESTATION OF HIS OR HER DISABILITY?

When is MDR required?

(4) (a): "If a disciplinary action is contemplated as described in paragraph (1) or paragraph (2) [see page 6] for a behavior of a child with a disability described in either of those paragraphs, or if a disciplinary action involving a change in placement for more than 10 days is contemplated for a child with a disability who has engaged in other behavior that violated any rule of code of conduct of the local educational agency that applies to all children."

"(I) no later than the date on which the decision to take action is made, the parents shall be notified of that decision and all procedural safeguards accorded under this section; and (ii) immediately if possible, but in no case later than 10 school days after the date on which the decision to take that action is made, a review shall be conducted of the relationship between the child's disability and the behavioral subject to the disciplinary action." [Section 615 (k) (4) (A)]

Who conducts the MDR?———————————————V

(4)(B) "INDIVIDUALS TO CARRY OUT REVIEW–A review described in subparagraph (A) [[see above, under "When."] shall be conducted by the IEP Team and other qualified personnel." [Section 615 (k) (4) (B)]

How is the MDR conducted?———————————V

(4) (C) 'CONDUCT OF REVIEW– In carrying out a review described in subparagraph (A), the IEP Team may determine that the behavior of the child was not [emphasis added] a manifestation of such child's disability only if the IEP Team–
   (i) first considers, in terms of behavior subject to disciplinary action, all relevant information, including - (I)evaluation and diagnostic results, including,

171

such results or other relevant information supplied by the parents of the child; (II) observations of the child, and (III) the child's IEP and placement, and

(ii) then determines that–(I) relationship to the behavior subject to disciplinary action, the child's IEP and placement were appropriate and the special education services, supplementary aids and services, and behavior intervention strategies were provided consistent with the child's IEP and placement; (II) the child's disability did not impair the ability of the child to understand the impact and consequences of the behavior subject to disciplinary action; and (III) the child's disability did not impair the ability of the child to control the behavior subject to disciplinary action." [Section 615 (k) (4) (C)

And then what happens?——————————————V

"(5) DETERMINATION THAT BEHAVIOR WAS NOT MANIFESTATION OF DISABILITY.–(A) IN GENERAL–If the results of the review described in paragraph (4) [A,B, &C, above] is a determination, consistent with paragraph (4) (C), that the behavior of the child with a disability was not a manifestation of the child's disability, the relevant disciplinary procedures applicable to, the relevant disciplinary procedures applicable to children without disability may be applied to the child in the same manner in which the children without disabilities may be applied to the child in the same manner in which they may be applied to children without disabilities, except as provided in section 612 (a) (1) [the requirement that schools provide FAPE to children with disabilities who have been suspended or expelled from school.]

"(B) ADDITIONAL REQUIREMENT–If the public agency initiates disciplinary procedures applicable to all children, the agency shall ensure that the special education and disciplinary records of the child with a disability are transmitted for consideration by the person or persons making the final determination regarding the disciplinary action" [Section 615 (k) (5)]

Parent appeal————————————————V

(6) "(A) IN GENERAL–(I) If the child's parent disagrees with a determination that the child's behavior was not a manifestation of the child's disability or with any decision regarding placement, the parent may request a hearing. (ii) The State or local educational agency shall arrange for an expedited hearing in any case described in this subsection when requested by a parent.

"(B) REVIEW OF DECISION–(I) In reviewing a decision with respect to the manifestation determination, the hearing officer shall determine whether the public agency has demonstrated that the child's behavior was not a manifestation of such child's disability consistent with the requirements of paragraph (4) (C) [see "(4) (C), Conduct of Review," on previous page].

"(ii) In reviewing a decision under paragraph (1) (A) (ii) [when school personnel change the child's placement for up to 45 days] to place the child in an interim alternative educational setting, the hearing officer shall apply the standards set out in paragraph (2)" [when a hearing officer orders a change in placement for not more than 45 days] [Section 615 (k) (6)].

Placement During Appeal——————————V

"(7) PLACEMENT DURING APPEALS

"(A) IN GENERAL–When a parent requests a hearing regarding a disciplinary action described in paragraph (1) (A) (ii) or paragraph (2) to challenge the interim alternative educational setting or the manifestation determination, the child shall remain in the interim alternative educational setting pending the decision of the hearing officer or until the expiration of the time period for in paragraph (1) (A) (ii) or paragraph (2), whichever occurs first, unless the parent and the State of local educational agency agree otherwise.

"(B) CURRENT PLACEMENT–If a child is placed in an interim alternative educational setting pursuant to paragraph (1) (A) (ii) or paragraph (2) and school personnel propose to change the child's placement after expiration of the interim alternative placement, during the pendency of any proceeding to challenge the proposed change in placement, the child shall remain in the current placement (the child's placement prior to the interim alternative educational setting), except as provided in subparagraph (C) [below].

"(C) EXPEDITED HEARING–(I) If school personnel maintain that it is dangerous for the child to be in the current placement (placement prior to removal to the interim alternative educational setting) during the pendency of the due process proceedings, the local educational agency may request an expedited hearing.

(iii) In determining whether the child may be placed in the alternative educational setting or in another appropriate placement ordered by the hearing officer, the hearing officer shall apply the standards set out in paragraph (2).

Referral to and action by law enforcement and judicial authorities——————V

(9) "(A) Nothing in this part shall be construed to prohibit an agency from reporting a crime committed by a child with a disability to appropriate authorities or to prevent State law enforcement and judicial authorities from exercising their responsibilities with regard to the application of Federal and State law to crimes committed by a child with a disability."

"(B) An agency reporting a crime committed by a child with a disability shall ensure that copies of the special education and disciplinary records of the child are transmitted for consideration by the appropriate authorities to whom it reports the crime." [Section 615 (k) (9) and (B)].

Appendix G

ABSTRACT

ED 417 536   EC 306 279

AUTHOR   Seltzer, Tammy
TITLE   Una Nueva IDEA: Una Guia para Padres acerca de los
                  Cambios en la Ley de Educacion Especial para Ninos con
                  Incapacidades (A New Idea: A Parentís Guide to the
                  Changes in Social Education Law for Children with
                  Disabilities)
INSTITUTION   Bazelon Center for Mental Health Law, Washington, DC
PUB DATE   1998-00-00
NOTE   25p.; Translated into Spanish from English language
                  version, see EC 306
                  278. Financial support also provided by the Center on
                  Crime, Communities, and Culture and the Lois and
                  Richard England Foundations.
AVAILABLE FROM   Bazzelon Center for Mental Health Law, 1101 15th Street,
                  N.W., Suite, 1212, Washington, DC 2005-5002; telephone:
                  (202) 467-5730; TDD: (202) 223-0409; e-mail: HN1660@
                  handsnet.org.; www.bazelon.org
PUB TYPE   Guides - Non-Classroom (055) – Translations (170)
LANGUAGE   Spanish
EDRS PRICE   MF01/PC01 Plus Postage.
DESCRIPTORS   Compliance (Legal); Decision Making; *Disabilities;
                  *Discipline; *Educational Legislation; Elementary
                  Secondary Education; Federal Legislation; Individualized
                  Education Programs; *Parent Participation; Parental
                  Rights; Parent School Relationship; Spanish; *Special
                  Education; Student Placement; Student Rights; Suspension
IDENTIFIERS   *Individuals with Disabilities Education Act Amend

ABSTRACT

This guide for parents, in Spanish, explains the changes in the federal special education law resulting from the 1997 amendments to the Individuals with Disabilities Education Act (IDEA). Changes related to the parent's role in decisions about the child's education and in how schools can discipline special education students are highlighted. A question-and-answer format is generally used throughout the guide. After a section summarizing the importance of parental involvement, the next section considers such topics as eligibility under IDEA, disagreements with the school regarding testing, and retesting requirements. Following a section on the parent's role in the placement decision, a section on writing the Individualized Education Program (IEP) offers tips for parent participation in IEP meetings, members of the IEP team, and placement decisions. The section on disciplining students is explained in questions and answers on suspensions of 10 days or less, requirements if the child is suspended for longer than 10 days, the requirement that schools conduct a "manifestation determination" (which determines whether the child's behavior was caused by or related to the disability), misbehavior involving weapons or drugs, and placement in an Interim Alternative Educational Setting. The final two sections summarize parental rights and identify related laws (Contains a listing of "words to know" and resources) (DB).

Appendix H

INTEREST SURVEY–PARENT WORKSHOPS

Please check topics that would be of most interest to you.

General Topics for Parents of Special Education Students

_____1. The Challenge of Being a Single Parent

_____2. Assertive Discipline–Creating a Positive Atmosphere at Home

_____3. Divorce and Separation–Effects on Families

_____4. Parent Roles in Sex Education

_____5. Stepfamilies–How to Live in One Successfully

_____6. Parent-Teacher Conferencing–Tips for Parents

_____7. Helping Children Build Good Study Habits

_____8. Getting the Help You Need When Your Child Has Problems in School

_____9. Self-Esteem–Helping Kids Feel Good About Themselves

_____10. Freedom and Control–Setting Limits for Children

_____11. Communicating with Children

_____12. Helping Your Child Develop Language

_____13. Spending Quality Time with Children

_____14. Home Activities for the Young Child

_____15. Living with Your Adolescent

_____16. Drug and Alcohol Use and Abuse

_____17. Helping Your Child Plan His/Her Future

_____18. Stresses of Parenting an Exceptional Child

_____19. Helping Siblings of the Disabled

_____20. Sex Education for the Disabled Individual

_____21. Helping the Learning Disabled Child

_____22. The IEP Process–Legal Issues and Parent Role

_____23. Behavior Management Techniques for Difficult Children

_____24. Dealing with Professionals: Teachers, Therapists, Diagnosticians, Principals

_____25. Your Child Has Been Referred to Special Education–What Does This Mean?

Glossary

AMENDED RAINE DECREE–Judicial decision which required the state to provide special education to school-age children with disabilities 5–20 (preceded P.L. 94-142).

ARCHITECTURAL BARRIERS–Those structural and physical obstructions which, merely by existing, exclude or discriminate against handicapped people, i.e., elevators, phone booths, etc.

ARD COMMITTEE–(Admission, Review, and Dismissal Committee) Required by state, not federal law and maintained by the LEA and comprised of individuals familiar with the child's current level of functioning (i.e., direct services deliverers, health department personnel, and a special educator. The ARD Committee refers for placement and reviews the individualized educational program of every child with disability.

ASSESSMENT–Extensive procedure given to all children who have been identified through screening as potentially in need of special education programs. It shall consist of reading, math, spelling, written and oral language, and perceptual motor functioning as appropriate. Cognitive, emotional, and physical factors shall also be assessed as appropriate. Each assessment report shall also include a description of the child's behavior which establishes the existence of a disabling condition; a statement which describes, in terms of special education services needed, the child's performance as it deviates from developmental milestones and/or general education objectives; a statement of criteria used to establish the deviation of the child's behaviors; and the signature of the assessor.

DUE PROCESS–A right to have any law applied reasonably and with sufficient safeguards, such as hearings and notice to ensure that an individual is dealt with fairly. A Due Process Hearing is held when there is disagreement between the parent and the educational agency (either local or state) as to the identification, evaluation, and/or placement of a child with a disability into a special education program. Parents have the right to present evidence, require the attendance of and cross-examine witnesses, and obtain independent assessments which must be considered.

EARLY IDENTIFICATION–Programs provided by LEAs for the preschool-age child who may be in need of special education services.

EVALUATION–An additional review of the child's program which occurs at least annually and is conducted to determine: (a) whether the child has achieved the goals set forth in his/her IEP, (b) whether the child has met the criteria which would indicate readiness to enter into a less restrictive/intensive special education program, and (c) whether the program of the child is in should be specifically modified so as to make it more suitable.

FAPE (Free Appropriate Public Education)–The federal phrase which describes the education to which children with disabilities are entitled.

FERPA (Family Education Rights and Privacy Act)–Also known as the Buckley Amendment, it permits parents to examine and copy (at reasonable cost) any and all material in the child's permanent record.

CHILDREN WITH DISABILITIES–Those children who have been determined through appropriate assessment as having temporary and long-term special education needs arising from cognitive, emotional, or physical factors or any combination of factors. Their ability to meet general educational objectives is impaired to such a degree that services in the general education programs are inadequate in preparing them to achieve their educational potential.

IEP (Individualized Education Program)–A written comprehensive outline for total special education services which describes the special education needs of the child and the services to be provided to meet those needs. It is developed in a collaborative meeting with LEA representatives, parents, teachers, the student, when appropriate, and all other persons having direct responsibilities for the implementation of the IEP. The IEP must be developed before placement, approved by the ARD Committee, signed by the parent, and implemented within 30 calendar days after development.

IHO (Impartial Hearing Officer)–Person who is knowledgeable in the fields and areas significant to the review of the child's education. Three IHOs preside at each state level hearing. (It can be one person at a local level hearing.) No person may serve as an IHO who is an employee of a local school system, an employee of an agency involved in the education or care of the child, an employee of the SEA, or a member of the State Board of Education. All IHOs in Maryland's State Level Hearings have completed a comprehensive training program.

LEA (Local Education Agency)–Also known as the LSS (Local School System), there are 24 in Maryland (the 23 counties and Baltimore City). The LEA is responsible for providing the actual education received.

LRE (Least Restrictive Environment)–The educational setting that is considered educationally appropriate, to the maximum extent possible with non-handicapped children.

NEGATIVE LANGUAGE –The term, when used with reference to an individual of limited English proficiency, means the language normally used by the individual or, in the case of the child, the language normally used by the parents of the child.

SEA (State Education Agency)–The SEA is responsible for monitoring the LEAs educational programs provided to children with disabilities.

INDEX

Note: Page numbers followed by a "t" indicate that the information is found in a table.

181